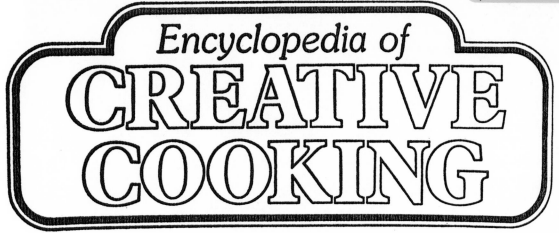

Encyclopedia of CREATIVE COOKING

Volume 5
Fish Cookery

Editors for U.S. editions
Steve Sherman and Julia Older

ECB Enterprises Inc.

All about Fish

Fish can add variety to your daily menu. There is a wide range of fish (and shellfish) to choose from, with many different tastes and textures, from the kings of fish, salmon and trout, through flat fish, halibut and sole, and oily fish, mackerel and herring, to the tiny sardines. Whether planning an everyday meal or a dinner party, there is always a fish to suit the occasion.

Your choice of fish will probably depend on the occasion and how much money you wish to spend but all fish, no matter what the cost, contain many vital nutrients. Fish is made up of protein, fat and water and also contains vitamins and minerals. For example, 8 ozs. herring contains: $23\frac{1}{2}$ g protein; $14\frac{1}{2}$ mg calcium; 200 i.u. vitamin A; 1300 i.u. vitamin D; 2 mg iron; 0.05 mg vitamin B.

Protein Cod is very rich in protein, particularly the liver and the roe. The protein content in salmon and trout is higher still, but a little lower in white fish. A rich egg sauce will increase the protein content in a white fish dish.

Fat The fat content in fish varies greatly according to species, and accounts for the wide variation in calories provided by fish. Fish of the cod family contain less than one percent fat while halibut has 2 to 5 percent fat. Fatty fish such as salmon, mackerel or herring are always relatively fatty but the fat content varies with the season and spawning cycle—herring can contain as little as 5 percent or as much as 22 percent fat. Fat in fish is not localized, as it is in meat, but is distributed throughout. In certain areas however, particularly just below the skin, the fat content is higher than elsewhere. The fat of fish is also easily digested.

Vitamins The flesh of fatty fish contains a little vitamin A and is rich in vitamin D. The lean fish have almost no vitamin A or D in the flesh. Fish oils, found in the liver, provide a reliable source of vitamins A and D — these vitamins are more concentrated in the livers of fatty species. Livers of halibut and tuna are especially rich in both vitamins A and D. Fish, like meat, is a good source of niacin and provides riboflavin as well. The proportions of the different vitamins vary with the species and a certain amount is lost in cooking.

Minerals All fish are good sources of phosphorous, iodine, copper and fluorine. Most of the calcium in fish is found in the bones and, for this reason, it is wise to include the softened bones when eating canned fish. The iron content of fish is rather low and the diet should provide other sources of this mineral. Shellfish, such as oysters and clams, which are eaten whole, provide more iron than other fish.

Fish is cooked and eaten all over the world, whether grilled over a primitive wood fire, or served in a delicious wine sauce with truffles by a great French chef. The supply of various kinds of fish and their abundance during different seasons of the year is reflected in the market price. Although prices of some fish are high during off-season periods or because of scarcity, on average, fish are an economical food source. Fish can be especially delicious if served with a rich wine sauce to add extra flavor.

Fish is not only nourishing and tasty but also more digestible than meat. To obtain the same benefit as from meat, fish should be eaten in larger quantities — 2 lbs. cod equals 1 lb. meat.

Whatever the method of preparation, fish nearly always tastes best when it is fresh from the sea. There are exceptions: sole is less tough if allowed to stand on ice for a day or two, and salmon will improve in flavor if kept on ice for several days.

Choosing and Buying Fish
The quality of fish is largely determined by its freshness. Always make sure that the fish you buy are fresh. Check that the skin is shiny and bright and the scales do not cling tightly. The gills should be a clear bright red, free from shine. They should not be pink, grey or brownish-green. The eyes should be bright, clear and full — not faded, cloudy or sunken. The flesh should be firm and elastic to the touch and should not separate easily from the bone. Above all, the fish should not smell strongly or unpleasantly — it should have only a mild, characteristic odor.

Methods of Cooking Fish
These depend on the nature of the fish and on the recipe. Sometimes a combination of several methods is required to complete one fish dish. The chief methods used are:

Boiling: applicable to large or small pieces, or whole fish, which are completely immersed in the cooking liquid.

Boil Point 'Au Bleu': the fish must be alive. It is cooked in clear stock with vinegar.

Poaching: the fish is placed in only a little liquid and the liquor is used as a base for the sauce.

Stewing: a form of poaching. Fish cooked in this way are served as soup in clear broth, or styled 'en matelote,' in which case the broth is thickened with a roux or cream.

Shallow frying: the fish is cooked with a little fat in a skillet. When cooked in clarified butter and finished with 'beurre noisette,' the method is called 'à la Meunière.'

Deep frying: the fish is completely immersed in fat or oil, usually coated in batter, crumbs or seasoned flour and milk.

Baking: the fish is baked in leaves or foil.

Roasting: cooked in the oven and basted with fat.

Braising: baked in the oven with a little liquor on a bed of root vegetables.

Grilling: cooked on a charcoal grill or broiler.

Au Gratin: the fish is cooked until the moisture has evaporated and the top is browned to form a crust.

In salted water: this procedure varies according to the size and cut of the fish. With whole fish, immerse in cold, salted water or court bouillon, bring to a boil and simmer until the fish is cooked. With cut fish, immerse the fish in boiling, salted water and simmer for a few minutes.

Saltwater Fish

Atlantic	Pacific
Alewives	Anchovies
Bass	Cod
Catfish	Flounder
Cod	Halibut
Cusk	Herring
Eels	Ling Cod
Flounder	Rockfish
Haddock	Salmon:
Hake	(Chum)
Halibut	(Cohoe)
Herring	(Pink)
Mackerel	(Spring)
Pollock	(Sockeye)
Ocean Perch	Skate
Salmon	Sole
Shad	Trout
Skate	Tuna:
Smelts	(Albacore)
Sole	
Swordfish	
Tuna	

Poached Fish

Poached Cod Andalouse

¼ cup butter
8 boneless cod steaks
pinch garlic salt, pepper, paprika
1 large onion, cut into rings
¼ cup red pepper, cut into strips
2 large white mushrooms, sliced
grated rind and juice 1 lemon
1 tablespoon white wine vinegar
⅔ cup water
1 chicken bouillon cube
1 branch celery, chopped
2 tablespoons tomato paste
1 bouquet garni
⅔ cup light cream or milk
1 tablespoon cornstarch

1 Preheat the oven to 400°F. Grease a shallow baking dish with half of the butter. Arrange the fish steaks in the dish and dot with small pieces of butter. Season with salt, pepper and paprika.

2 Place the onion rings, strips of red pepper and sliced mushrooms on the fish steaks. Sprinkle with grated lemon, lemon juice and vinegar.

3 Place the wine, water, bouillon cube, chopped celery and tomato paste in a saucepan and boil for 2 minutes. Pour over the fish steaks.

4 Place a bouquet garni on the side and bake in the preheated oven for 18 minutes.

5 Pour the fish liquid into a small saucepan and bring to a boil. Boil for 5 minutes.

6 Blend together the cream and cornstarch. Pour into the boiling

fish stock, stirring all the time until it thickens. Cook for 5 minutes. Coat the fish evenly with the sauce and serve.

Serves 4

Poached Cod Andalouse — a delicious way of serving cod in a wine sauce flavored with red pepper, mushrooms and onions

Red Mullet Breton-style

6 fillets medium-size mullet
1 chicken bouillon cube
1⅔ cups water
6 tablespoons dry white wine
¼ cup butter
white parts 2 leeks, sliced
2 onions, chopped
½ cup flour
⅞ cup light cream
3 sprigs parsley, chopped

1 Preheat the oven to 375°F. Prepare the stock from the cube and hot water. Butter a flameproof dish

and place the fillets of fish on it. Add the stock and white wine and cover with a sheet of aluminum foil.

2 Bring to a boil over high heat, then cook for 8 minutes in the oven. Adjust the seasoning. Remove the fish to a deep serving dish and keep hot.

3 Heat the butter in a pan and cook the leeks and onions until lightly browned. Add the flour and stir well with a wooden spoon for 5 minutes over low heat.

4 Pour 1⅓ cups of the stock into the pan. Stir until blended and cook 5 minutes longer. Then incorporate the cream and cook carefully for 3 minutes.

5 Pour the sauce over the fish and sprinkle with the chopped parsley.

Serves 6

Fillet of Sole Melone

1 medium onion, chopped
$\frac{1}{4}$ cup butter
four 3-oz. sole fillets
pinch salt and pepper
pinch ground ginger
grated rind and juice 1 lemon
$\frac{2}{3}$ cup water
1 chicken bouillon cube
$\frac{2}{3}$ cup light cream
$\frac{1}{2}$ honeydew melon, peeled and
   deseeded
1 tablespoon cornstarch
3 medium potatoes, cooked and
   mashed
1 egg yolk
2 tablespoons butter
salt and pepper
1 egg, beaten
chopped parsley

1 Preheat the oven to 400°F. Butter a shallow dish and sprinkle the bottom with the chopped onion.

2 Pound the fish fillets lightly with a rolling pin — to break down the fibers — then season with salt, pepper and ground ginger. Fold the fillets in two and place in the shallow dish. Add the grated lemon rind and lemon juice, the water and crumbled chicken bouillon cube. Cover with a piece of parchment paper.

3 Bake on the top shelf of the preheated oven for 15 minutes. When cooked, pour the fish stock into a small saucepan. Leave the oven at the same temperature.

4 Boil the fish liquor for 3 minutes and thicken it with the cream and cornstarch which have been blended together. Season.

Fillet of Sole Melone, served with a salad of lettuce, hard-boiled eggs, red pepper, celery, carrot and raisins

5 Cut the melon into small cubes.

6 Blend the mashed potatoes with the egg yolk and butter and season. Place in a piping bag and pipe an attractive border around a clean, shallow dish. Dry the potatoes in the oven for 6 minutes. Then brush with beaten egg. Arrange the cooked fish and raw melon cubes in the center and pour on the cream sauce. Brown in the oven for 8 minutes. Decorate with melon balls and parsley.

Serves 4

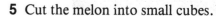

Cod Dugleré

2 tablespoons chopped onions
four $\frac{1}{2}$-lb. cod steaks
salt and pepper
3 chopped, peeled tomatoes
$\frac{1}{4}$ cup soft butter
$\frac{2}{3}$ cup dry white wine
$\frac{1}{3}$ cup fish stock
1 bay leaf
pinch tarragon
juice $\frac{1}{2}$ lemon
pinch cayenne pepper
1 tablespoon chopped parsley

1 Preheat the oven to 400°F. Butter a shallow dish and sprinkle with the chopped onions. Place the cod on top and season with salt and pepper.

2 Cover with the coarsely chopped tomatoes and dot with half of the butter.

3 Pour the stock and the wine over the fish. Add the bay leaf and tarragon.

4 Bake in the preheated oven for 15-20 minutes.

5 Pour the sauce into a saucepan and boil to reduce by half. Season well and add the lemon juice and cayenne pepper.

6 Remove from the heat and stir in the remaining soft butter to cream it.

7 Pour the sauce over the fish and garnish with chopped parsley.

Serves 4

Flounder Belomar

1 lb. flounder fillets
juice ½ lemon
pinch salt
2 tablespoons butter
2 onions, chopped

1¼ cups sliced, white mushrooms
1 cup chopped dill pickles
¼ cup brandy (optional)
3 tablespoons tomato paste
⅔ cup light cream
freshly ground black pepper

1 Rub the flounder fillets with the lemon juice and lightly sprinkle them with salt.

2 Heat the butter and add the onions and mushrooms. Sauté over low heat.

3 Add the dill pickles and pour in the brandy. Ignite and let the flames die down.

*Flounder Belomar —
fillets of fish served in
a rich creamy sauce, flavored
with brandy*

4 Stir in the tomato paste and cream. Season with salt and pepper.

5 Fold over the flounder fillets and put them in the sauce. Cover and simmer for 10 minutes.

6 Pour into a serving dish and serve with boiled rice or potatoes.

Serves 4

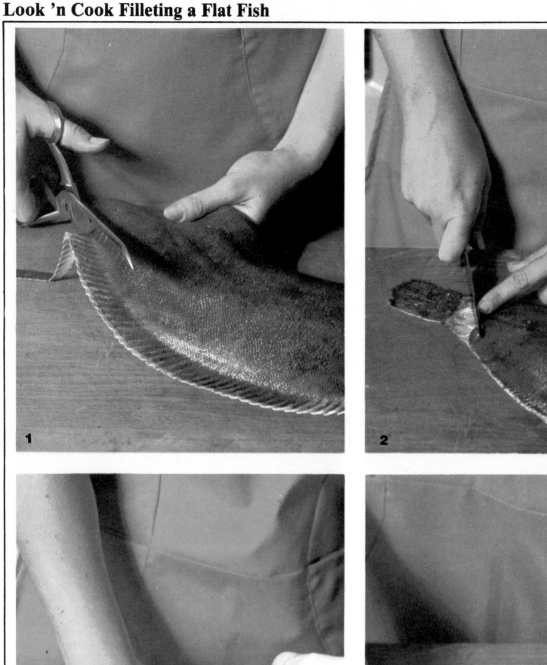

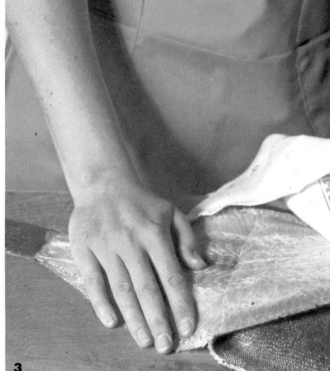

1 Cut off the fins on both sides with a pair of very sharp scissors **2** Slice through the black skin near the tail. Lift and scrape with the point of a knife to separate the skin from the flesh **3** Take hold of the skin with a tea towel and, keeping the sole flat, tear off the skin. Pull from the tail to the head **4** Slip the blade of a knife between the slightly pink edges and the white fillets **5** Separate the two fillets by drawing the knife

point along the backbone **6** Lift the fillets by slipping the knife underneath. Make small cuts from the backbone toward the edge on both sides **7** Lightly press the fillets to flatten them **8** The fillets can then be rolled up (paupiettes) or folded over according to the recipe used. Never throw away the fish bones — they can be used in making stock

Fillet of Sole Villeroy

1 clove garlic
1 whole clove
heads and trimmings of several
  sole
1 onion, thinly sliced
1 carrot, thinly sliced
bouquet garni
1 cup dry white wine
salt and pepper
8 fillets of sole
3 tablespoons butter
6 tablespoons flour
pinch grated nutmeg
2 eggs plus 2 egg yolks
$\frac{1}{4}$ cup sour cream
3 tablespoons oil
oil for deep frying
2 cups dried breadcrumbs

1 Peel the garlic, and stick the clove into it.

2 Put the heads and fish trimmings, onion and carrot slices, bouquet garni, garlic stuck with clove, half the white wine and $1\frac{1}{4}$ cups water into a saucepan. Season with salt and pepper and leave to simmer gently for 25 minutes.

3 Preheat the oven to 425°F.

4 Butter an ovenproof dish.

5 Season the fillets of sole with salt and pepper. Fold each in half with the skin inside. Place on the buttered dish. Pour the rest of the white wine over the fish and cook in the oven for 6 or 7 minutes.

6 As soon as the fillets have stiffened a little, drain them and put them on a plate.

7 Pour the cooking juice into the fish stock.

8 Strain the fish stock.

9 Heat 3 tablespoons butter in a saucepan over low heat. Add the flour, stirring with a wooden spoon. Cook for a few minutes, then gradually add the fish stock, mixing continuously to form a smooth thick sauce. Then add the grated nutmeg and simmer for 5 minutes.

10 Blend the egg yolks with the cream, and add to the sauce, stirring with a wooden spoon. Heat the sauce for 3 or 4 minutes until it is very thick but do not boil. Take off the heat and cool.

11 Grease your work surface with 1 tablespoon of the oil.

12 When the sauce is almost cold, coat the sole fillets with it.

13 Place the sauce-coated fillets on the work surface and cool. The sauce should be firm and not stick to the fingers.

14 Heat the oil in a deep fat fryer to 375°F.

15 Break the remaining 2 eggs into a bowl, and beat in the rest of the oil.

16 Heat a serving dish.

17 Dip the fillets of sole first into the beaten eggs, then into the breadcrumbs. Gently press the breadcrumbs into place.

18 Lower the fillets into the hot oil. Fry until golden and then drain.

19 Arrange the fillets of sole on the serving dish and serve immediately with a tomato sauce.

Serves 4

Poached Haddock with Herbs

1½ lbs. smoked haddock
1 cup milk
1 small bunch chervil
1 small bunch parsley
1 small bunch tarragon
1 hard-boiled egg, finely chopped
juice 3 lemons
1 teaspoon heavy cream
salt and pepper

6 tablespoons butter
few sprigs parsley

1 Put the haddock in a pan. Add the milk and enough cold water to cover the fish, then simmer for 15 minutes.

2 Meanwhile, mince the herbs and put in a bowl with the chopped egg. Stir well to mix.

3 Put the lemon juice and cream in a small pan. Season with salt and pepper. Bring to a boil, then add the butter in small pieces, beating constantly with a whisk. Remove from the heat and stir in the egg and herb mixture. Keep hot.

4 Drain the haddock carefully and arrange the fish on a warm serving dish. Garnish with parsley and serve immediately. Serve the herb sauce separately.

Serves 4

Boiled Flounder

four 10-oz. flounder fillets
juice 1 lemon
2 tablespoons salt
parsley sprigs

1 Preheat the oven to 400°F.

2 Rub the fish with lemon juice and place in a shallow baking dish. Cover with water and add the salt.

3 Bring to a boil on top of the stove and then place in the oven to simmer for 20 minutes.

4 Garnish with sprigs of parsley and serve with boiled potatoes and Hollandaise sauce.

Serves 4

Tip: To enhance the delicate flavor of flounder, always serve it with a sauce such as Hollandaise or shrimp sauce. Halibut can be boiled and served in the same way.

Fillet of Flounder Tivoli

four ¼-lb. fillets of flounder, sliced
  into small pieces
½ cup flour
pinch salt and pepper
¼ cup oil
½ cup sliced, white leeks
⅓ cup chopped, skinned tomatoes
2 chopped mint leaves
1 pinch ground thyme
⅔ cup cider

3 tablespoons tomato paste
1 chicken bouillon cube
pinch dill

1 Wash and drain the fish fillets
and sprinkle with seasoned flour.

2 Heat the oil in a skillet and fry
the fish fillets for 3 minutes. Remove and keep warm.

3 Add the leeks and sauté for 3
minutes. Add the chopped tomatoes, mint, thyme, cider, tomato
paste and bouillon cube and stir

*Fillet of Flounder Tivoli prepared
in a tangy apple cider sauce, with
tomatoes and leeks to complement
the delicate flavor of the flounder*

well. Boil for 5 minutes to reduce
the liquid. Season well.

4 Reheat the fish fillets and place
on a warm serving dish. Pour on
the sauce and serve with a sprinkling of dill.

Serves 4

Fish Stocks & Sauces

Fish Stocks and Sauces

When making fish stock, do not use the bones of oily fish, which are not suitable for white sauces. A fish stock must be neutral with a sweetish taste. Sautéeing bones and onions in clarified butter produces a good flavor but tends to color the sauce.

Fish sauces must always be more acidic than those served with meat and poultry. This can be done by adding the juice of 1 lemon per 4½ cups of sauce and also some dry white wine — sweet wine tends to make the sauce grey in color. White wine vinegar is always preferable to cider vinegar when used with fish stock.

Basic Fish Stock

1 lb. fish heads, bones and
 trimmings
2 tablespoons butter
2 tablespoons oil
1 carrot, sliced
1 onion, sliced
3⅔ cups water
1¼ cups dry white wine
bouquet garni
pinch salt and pepper
1 chicken bouillon cube

1 Wash the fish heads and trimmings well.

2 Heat the butter and oil in a large pan and add the sliced carrot and onion. Cover and cook gently for 5 minutes.

3 Add the fish trimmings to the vegetables in the pan. Cook for 5 minutes.

4 Pour in the water and wine and add the bouquet garni. Season. Cook for 15 minutes.

5 Crumble in the bouillon cube and simmer for 5 minutes.

6 Strain through clean cheesecloth or a fine strainer, cover and cool. Refrigerate until required.

Makes 3⅔ cups

Tip: Fish stock should always be used the same day or frozen.

Basic White Wine Sauce

2 tablespoons butter
¼ cup flour
2½ cups fish stock
½ cup chopped shallots
⅔ cup dry white wine
4 egg yolks
⅔ cup light cream
pinch salt and pepper
pinch cayenne pepper
juice ½ lemon

1 Melt the butter in a saucepan and stir in the flour. Cook the roux for 3 minutes.

2 Add the fish stock gradually, stirring all the time, until the velouté sauce is smooth. Simmer for 20 minutes.

3 Boil the shallots in the wine until soft and add to the velouté sauce. Simmer for 15 minutes.

4 Blend the egg yolks with the cream and some of the sauce until well mixed. Pour into the velouté sauce and reheat, but do not allow the sauce to boil.

5 Season with salt and pepper and stir in the cayenne pepper and lemon juice.

Makes about 3⅔ cups

Fillet of Cod Véronique

four 6-oz. fillets of cod
pinch salt and pepper
¼ cup butter
⅔ cup dry white wine
1¼ cups velouté sauce
¼ cup light cream
pinch cayenne
juice ½ lemon
⅓ lb. skinned and split
 seedless green grapes

1 Preheat the oven to 400°F.

2 Wash and dry the cod fillets. Season with salt and the pepper.

3 Butter a shallow baking dish and arrange the fish fillets in it, side by side.

4 Pour in the dry white wine and velouté sauce, and cover with damp parchment paper.

5 Bake in the oven for 15 minutes. Remove the paper and pour off the liquor into a saucepan. Keep the fish warm.

6 Boil the liquor to reduce by half and stir in the cream, whisking all the time. Season with salt, pepper and cayenne and stir in the lemon juice.

7 Arrange the fish in a clean shallow dish. Pour on the sauce, and decorate with a border of grapes.

Serves 4

Tips: A fish sauce should always be made with ingredients which will enhance the flavor of the fish used. Aromatic herb sauces are best with oily fish such as sardines, trout or mackerel. The best stock you can make for a fish sauce is usually made from the liquid in which the fish is poached. A fish liquor of wine and onions infused with a bouquet garni can constitute the base for a delicious sauce. Thicken with a mixture of egg yolks and cream, or simply blend with a basic white sauce.

1 As a preliminary to making Poached Fish (see p. 402) make the fish stock. Ingredients: fish trimmings, butter, carrot, onion, white wine, bouquet garni, salt and pepper **2** Wash the fish and cut off heads, bones and trimmings **3** Heat some butter and oil in a large pan.

Add the carrots and onions and cook for 5 minutes. Add the fish trimmings and cook another 5 minutes **4** Add the water and wine and bouquet garni. Cook for 15 minutes, then crumble in the bouillon cube. Simmer 5 minutes

Braised Fish

Haddock with Anchovies

3 lbs. haddock
salt and pepper
6 canned anchovy fillets, drained
$\frac{1}{2}$ cup fine breadcrumbs
6 tablespoons soft butter
1 tablespoon chopped parsley
grated rind 1 lemon

1 Preheat the oven to 400°F.

2 Clean and wash the fish. Season with salt. Make several small incisions across the backbone of the fish with a sharp knife. Cut the anchovy fillets into thin strips and place in the slits.

3 Place the fish in a greased baking dish and sprinkle with the breadcrumbs. Melt 2 tablespoons butter and baste the fish.

4 Bake the fish for 20 minutes, basting it occasionally.

5 Cream the chopped parsley with the remaining butter and the grated lemon rind. Season with salt and pepper. Place in the refrigerator until firm but still pliable. Turn onto a sheet of aluminum foil and roll into a cylindrical shape. Refrigerate again. When really cold, cut into thin, round slices.

6 Serve the fish with the rounds of parsley butter and coleslaw tossed in a vinaigrette dressing.

Serves 4

Haddock with Anchovies — served with a salad of finely grated carrot, white cabbage and beets tossed in French dressing

Fillet of Sole Bonne Femme

6 tablespoons butter
$\frac{1}{4}$ cup chopped shallots
1 tablespoon chopped parsley
$1\frac{1}{4}$ cups sliced, white mushrooms
$\frac{1}{4}$ lb. fillets of sole
salt and pepper
$\frac{2}{3}$ cup dry white wine
$\frac{1}{3}$ cup fish stock
$\frac{2}{3}$ cup velouté sauce
juice $\frac{1}{2}$ lemon
pinch cayenne pepper

1 Preheat oven to 400°F.

2 Butter a shallow baking dish with 1 tablespoon butter. Sprinkle with the chopped shallots, parsley and sliced mushrooms.

3 Season the fillets of sole with salt and pepper and arrange them in the baking dish.

4 Add the wine, fish stock and

velouté sauce and heat the dish on top of the stove until the liquor is boiling.

5 Cover the dish and place in the oven for 8 minutes.

6 Keeping the fillets warm, pour the liquor into a pan and boil to reduce by one-third.

7 Cut the butter into small pieces and whisk it in, one piece at a time, until it is all blended and the liquor is creamy.

8 Check the seasoning and add the lemon juice.

9 Place the fish on an overproof serving platter and cover with the sauce. Sprinkle with cayenne pepper and place under the broiler for a few seconds to brown it. Decorate with sautéed mushrooms.

Serves 4

Tip: To make Sole Bercy, a delicious alternative to Sole Bonne Femme, just follow the recipe as indicated but omit the mushrooms.

Fillet of Lemon Sole Stockholm

¼ **cup butter**
2 tablespoons chopped onions
four 6-oz. fillets of lemon sole
salt and pepper
pinch paprika
⅔ **cup dry white wine**
1¼ **cups velouté sauce**
⅓ **cup light cream**
pinch dill
8 peeled, cooked shrimp

1 Preheat the oven to 400°F.

2 Grease a shallow baking dish with butter and sprinkle with chopped onions.

3 Arrange the fish fillets in the dish and season with salt, pepper and paprika.

Fillet of Lemon Sole Stockholm, cooked in white wine and cream, and served with whole shrimp and buttered rice

4 Add the wine, cover with a sheet of parchment paper and bake for 15 minutes.

5 Pour off the fish liquor into a pan and stir in the velouté sauce and cream. Cook over low heat, stirring constantly, for 10 minutes.

6 Check the seasoning and pour on the fish. Sprinkle with dill and garnish with the peeled shrimp. Serve with buttered, boiled rice.

Serves 4

Tip: Baking with dry heat is impossible for fish, thus no fish can be 'baked' without a certain amount of moisture. Always remember to add sufficient moisture to make up the loss from evaporation during the cooking process. To ensure that the moisture is retained either baste occasionally or cover the fish with foil or parchment paper.

Cod Manuella

eight ¼-lb. cod fillets
¼ cup flour
salt and pepper
¼ cup oil
1 onion, chopped
1 zucchini, peeled and sliced
3 tomatoes, peeled and chopped
1 red pepper, seeded and
   chopped
1 tablespoon tomato paste
1 tablespoon wine vinegar
⅔ cup dry sherry
⅔ cup water
1 chicken bouillon cube
pinch garlic salt
1 tablespoon chopped parsley

1 Clean and wash the cod fillets and cut into small pieces. Season the flour and sprinkle it over the cod.

2 Heat the oil and sauté the onion, sliced zucchini, chopped tomatoes and red pepper until soft (about 8 minutes).

3 Stir in the tomato paste, vinegar, sherry and water. Crumble in the bouillon cube and boil for 12 minutes, stirring from time to time.

4 Place the fish fillets on top. Season with salt and pepper and cover with a lid. Simmer gently on top of the stove for 12 minutes.

5 Pour into a serving dish and sprinkle with chopped parsley.

Serves 4

Cod Manuella — a Spanish dish in which cod is poached with zucchini, tomatoes and red peppers in a delicious sherry sauce

Fish Stuffings

Both stuffings are enough for 4 whole small fish or 4–6 fillets.

Mousseline Stuffing

1 cup raw finely ground cod
1 egg white
⅓ cup heavy cream
salt and pepper

1 Mix the fish paste with the egg white in a bowl. Place inside a larger bowl containing crushed ice and chill for at least 1 hour.

2 Add the heavy cream gradually, stirring all the time, then season with salt and pepper.

Herb and Breadcrumb Stuffing

1 cup coarsely ground haddock
1 tablespoon chopped parsley
1 small onion, grated
1 cup fresh white breadcrumbs
1 whole egg
salt and pepper
pinch of garlic salt

1 Mix the ground fish, chopped parsley, grated onion and breadcrumbs together.

2 Blend with the beaten egg and season with salt and pepper and the garlic salt. Use as a stuffing for any fish — whole round or flat fish and fillets.

1 Wash the cod, cutting along the backbone to fillet it **2** Remove the skin from the fillets **3** Chop up the flesh in a food mill or blender to obtain a very fine paste. Season with salt and pepper **4** Place the fish paste in a bowl and blend with the egg white. Put this bowl in another larger bowl full of crushed ice. Chill the mixture for at least an hour **5** and **6** Add the heavy cream, spoonful by spoonful, to the mousseline stuffing. Mix thoroughly with a wooden spoon **7** Flatten the fillets with a wooden mallet or rolling pin or a wide-

bladed knife. Season them, turn over and repeat the flattening process **8** Spread the stuffing over the fillets **9** Roll the fillets up from the tail end. Do not squeeze them—the stuffing will ooze out **10** Tie the stuffed fillets with string. Make 2 turns and one knot **11** Butter an ovenproof dish and sprinkle with chopped shallots.

Place the stuffed fillets, upright and tightly packed, on top **12** Pour in the white wine and fish stock. Cover with a lid or aluminum foil and cook for 20 minutes in the oven. Remove the string. Make a sauce with the fish liquor and eggs. Pour over the stuffed fillets and serve.

Stuffed Fillet of Sole with White Wine Sauce (Paupiettes de Sole)

For the Stuffing:
1 slice bread
½ lb. haddock fillets
6 tablespoons butter
pinch grated nutmeg
1 egg, beaten
salt and pepper

For the Sauce:
eight 3-oz. fillets of sole
2 tablespoons chopped shallots
1 cup dry white wine
1 cup fish stock
1 tablespoon butter
2 tablespoons flour
2 egg yolks
juice 1 lemon
salt and pepper

1 Soak the bread in a little water and mash it with a fork. Put the haddock fillets through a food mill or in a blender. (If using a blender, add 1-2 tablespoons water or milk.)

2 Heat 2 tablespoons butter in a small saucepan and add the soaked, crumbled bread. Stir with a wooden spoon until blended but do not brown.

3 Melt the remainder of the butter in a small saucepan over low heat.

4 In a bowl mix the ground haddock and breadcrumb mixture. Add the melted butter, grated nutmeg, beaten egg, and season with salt and pepper. Blend well together.

5 Preheat the oven to 400°F.

6 Flatten the fillets of sole on both sides with a wooden mallet or a rolling pin. (First place the fish between two pieces of parchment paper or foil, so that it does not stick to the board or the mallet.) Then season them with salt and pepper.

7 Spread the stuffing over the fillets and roll them up from the tail end. Be careful not to squeeze them, or the stuffing will ooze out. Tie them with string.

8 Butter a small, round ovenproof dish (about 6 inches in diameter) and sprinkle with the chopped shallots. Arrange the stuffed fillets on top, standing upright and packed in tightly, very close to each other.

9 Pour on the wine and fish stock. Cover with a lid or aluminum foil and cook in the oven for about 20 minutes.

10 Blend the butter and flour together to make a firm paste.

11 Remove the string from the stuffed fillets. Arrange them on a serving dish and keep warm.

12 Pour off the fish liquor into a saucepan and boil to reduce by one third. Add the butter paste (*beurre manié*), a little at a time, stirring constantly to make a thick, smooth sauce.

13 Beat the egg yolks with the lemon juice and add to the sauce.

Adjust the seasoning. Heat gently over low heat, stirring constantly until the sauce coats the back of the spoon. Do not allow it to boil.

14 Pour the sauce over the stuffed fillets. Serve with crescents of puff pastry (*fleurons*) and baked potatoes or plain rice.

Serves 4

Tip: Lemon sole or flounder could both be substituted for sole in this dish. Also, a mousseline stuffing could be used, as shown in the step-by-step picture sequence, instead of the coarser breadcrumb-based stuffing.

Fillets of Sole, paupiette style, may be stuffed with a mixture of either breadcrumbs and fish or ground haddock and cream

Fish and Wine

Poached Flounder

3 lbs. flounder
¼ cup butter
¼ cup chopped shallots
1 tablespoon freshly chopped
 mixed tarragon, parsley, chives,
 mint

For the Fish Stock:
2 tablespoons butter
2 tablespoons oil
1 carrot, sliced
1 onion, sliced
1¼ cups water
1¼ cups dry white wine
bouquet garni
1 chicken bouillon cube

For the Sauce:
2 tablespoons cornstarch
⅔ cup heavy cream
2 egg yolks
2 tablespoons butter
salt and pepper
juice ½ lemon
pinch cayenne pepper

1 Preheat the oven to 400°F. Fillet and skin the fish. Wash the fillets and cut them into suitably sized portions. Heavily butter the bottom of a shallow ovenproof dish and sprinkle in the chopped shallot and the herbs. Place the fish pieces on top.

2 Make the fish stock: heat the butter and oil together in a pan, add the carrot and onion, cover and cook gently for 5 minutes. Wash the fish bones, skin and head, add them to the vegetables and cook for 5 minutes more. Stir in the water and wine and add the bouquet garni. Cook the stock for a further 15 minutes, then crumble in the bouillon cube. Simmer for 5 minutes and then strain the stock over the fish pieces. Cover with buttered parchment paper and bake in the preheated oven for 15 minutes.

3 Remove the dish from the oven, discard the parchment paper and lift out the pieces of fish with a slotted spoon. Arrange the fish on a serving dish and keep it warm.

4 Strain the fish stock into a pan and place over high heat. Boil for 8 minutes until reduced by half.

5 Make the stock: mix the cornstarch with the cream and add to the reduced stock, whisk continuously. Heat gently until the sauce thickens slightly, stirring all the time. Take the pan off the heat and whisk in the egg yolks and the butter, cut into small pieces. Whisk until the ingredients are well incorporated. Season the sauce with salt and pepper and add the lemon juice and cayenne pepper.

6 Pour the sauce over the fish pieces and place under a hot broiler for a few minutes to brown the top. Serve with boiled new potatoes, cauliflower or asparagus tips.

Serves 6

Tips: If any of the sauce is left over, try blending it with an equal quantity of white sauce and using this to cover mild-flavored vegetables such as cauliflower, leeks, celery, turnips. You can also use it with hard-boiled eggs and with rice.

Many types of fish can be used for this dish, including sole, salmon, cod and tuna. But make sure that you always use dry white wine and fresh herbs.

This dish can also be served cold: allow to cool and blend the sauce with a quarter as much mayonnaise or salad dressing. Place the fish on a bed of sliced cold cooked potato and pour on the sauce. Decorate with fresh lettuce leaves, tomatoes and cucumber.

Norwegian Baked Cod with Peppers

1 lb. cod fillet
salt and pepper
grated rind and juice ½ lemon
⅔ cup dry white wine
½ green pepper
½ sweet red pepper
¼ cup tomato paste
2 tablespoons flour
½ cup light cream
1 onion, chopped
2 cloves garlic, chopped
pinch paprika
pinch chopped thyme
½ cup Cheddar or Parmesan cheese
2 tablespoons fresh breadcrumbs

1 Preheat the oven to 400°F. Cut the fish into ½-inch slices and place them in an ovenproof dish. Season the fish with salt and pepper and add the lemon juice and white wine. Remove the membranes and seeds from the peppers and cut the fish into strips. Place the strips on top of the fish.

2 Mix together the tomato paste, grated lemon rind, flour, cream, chopped onion, chopped garlic, paprika and chopped thyme. Pour the mixture over the fish.

3 Sprinkle the fish with the cheese and breadcrumbs and bake in the preheated oven for 20-25 minutes.

Serves 4

1 To prepare the fish stock, see page 395. Remove the dish from the oven and discard the parchment paper **2** Lift the fish pieces from the stock using a slotted spoon and arrange them on a warm serving dish. Keep them warm **3** Pour the fish stock through a strainer into a saucepan and place over high heat. Boil for 8 minutes until the stock is reduced to half the original quantity **4** Blend the cornstarch with the heavy cream and add this mixture to the reduced stock, whisking all the time. Warm gently, until the sauce thickens slightly **5** Remove the pan from the heat and allow the sauce to cool a little. Cut the butter into small pieces and add them to the sauce with the egg yolks. Whisk until all the ingredients are well blended and the butter has completely melted **6** Spoon the thickened sauce over the fish pieces on the serving dish **7** Finally, place the dish under a hot broiler for a few minutes to brown the top

Fish Couscous

3 cups couscous
$\frac{1}{4}$ cup butter
$\frac{1}{2}$ cup oil
$\frac{1}{2}$ lb. perch, cleaned
1 lb. frozen squid (or shrimp)
1 clove garlic, chopped
1 medium onion, chopped
3 cups water
1$\frac{1}{4}$ cups dry white wine
bouquet garni
$\frac{1}{4}$ cup tomato paste
salt and pepper
pinch basil and chopped mint
pinch cayenne pepper or 2 red chili
    peppers, chopped
2 tablespoons cornstarch

1 Mix the couscous with the butter and 2 tablespoons oil in a bowl.

2 Wash the fish and cut each into 4 pieces across the bone. Cut the squid into 2-inch strips.

3 Heat the rest of the oil in a large sauté pan, add the fish and squid and brown for 5 minutes. Add the garlic and onion, stir well and cook for 2 minutes. Pour in the water and wine and add the bouquet garni, tomato paste and seasonings. Bring to a boil and simmer for 20 minutes.

4 Discard the bouquet garni; place the fish in a shallow dish. Season to taste.

5 Boil half the fish stock. Mix the cornstarch with $\frac{1}{2}$ cup water and add it to the boiling stock. Cook until the stock clears and is slightly thickened. Season to taste and pour half the stock over the fish. Serve the rest as a sauce.

6 Preheat the oven to 400°F. Place the couscous in a pan with 2$\frac{1}{2}$ cups of the remaining fish stock and boil for 10 minutes. Season to taste and transfer to an ovenproof dish. Place the couscous in the oven for about 8 minutes to dry.

Couscous is a North African dish of semolina and meat, poultry or fish. Here perch and squid make up our fish couscous, but other varieties may be substituted

7 Serve the fish, sauce, and couscous in separate dishes.

Serves 4

Fish-balls with Vegetables

1 lb. cod
2 tablespoons chopped onion
1 cup fresh breadcrumbs
salt and pepper
1 egg, beaten
1$\frac{1}{4}$ cups water
scant 1 tablespoon cornstarch
    blended with $\frac{1}{2}$ cup water
1 tablespoon soy sauce
1 sweet red pepper, seeded and
    chopped
2 tablespoons oil
$\frac{1}{2}$ lb. sliced mushrooms
1 lb. bean sprouts
1 tablespoon chopped parsley

1 Preheat the oven to 400°F. Grind the fish, onion and breadcrumbs together. Season, bind with the egg and form into about 20 balls.

2 Place the fish-balls in a greased shallow dish, cover with the water and place in the oven for 15 minutes.

3 Lift the balls from the stock and keep them warm. Pour the stock into a skillet and boil for 5 minutes. Add the cornstarch and cook for a few minutes more. Season and add the soy sauce, red pepper and fish-balls. Cook for 5 minutes longer.

4 Heat the oil in a separate pan and sauté the mushrooms and bean sprouts for 2-3 minutes. Add them to the fish-balls, sprinkle with the parsley and serve.

Serves 4

Fish-balls with Vegetables — ground white fish with bean sprouts, peppers and mushrooms

Fish Curry

1 lb. haddock fillet
⅔ cup milk and water, mixed
salt and black pepper
¼ cup butter
1 small onion, finely chopped
¼ cup flour
¼ cup curry powder
⅔ cup dry white wine
1 tablespoon lemon juice
2 tablespoons raisins
1 tablespoon mango chutney
1 tablespoon shredded coconut
6 ozs. peeled, deveined shrimp
1 small green pepper, seeded
   and chopped

1 Place the fish in a pan with the milk and water, add seasoning and 2 tablespoons of the butter. Bring to a boil and poach gently for a few minutes. Remove the fish, reserving the stock, and keep the fish warm.

2 Melt the remaining butter in a pan, add the onion and fry gently until softened. Stir in the flour and curry powder and cook for 1-2 minutes.

3 Make up the reserved fish stock to 2 cups with the wine and more water. Gradually blend this liquid into the curry mixture, then cook until thickened, stirring well.

4 Add the lemon juice, raisins, chutney and coconut, and then most of the shrimp and green pepper, reserving a few shrimp and a little pepper for decoration. Heat through.

5 Divide the fish into 4 portions and place them on a serving dish. Pour the sauce over the top and decorate with the reserved shrimp

Fish Curry and accompaniments — saffron rice with peanuts and tomato and onion slices

and pepper. Serve with saffron rice with peanuts.

Serves 4

Saffron Rice with Peanuts

¼ cup oil
1 small onion, chopped
1 cup long grain rice
4¼ cups water
1 bay leaf
1 chicken bouillon cube
pinch saffron
salt and pepper
⅓ cup roasted peanuts

1 Preheat the oven to 400°F. Heat the oil in a sauté pan, add the onion and cook for 2 minutes without browning. Stir in the rice and cook for 1 minute more until the rice is translucent.

2 Put the water, bay leaf, bouillon cube and saffron in a pan, bring to a boil and simmer for 5 minutes. Strain the stock into the pan and boil for a further 5 minutes. Transfer the contents of the pan to a shallow ovenproof dish, cover with a lid or parchment paper and bake in the preheated oven for 20 minutes.

3 Season the rice with salt and pepper, sprinkle with the roasted peanuts and serve.

Serves 4

Tip: If saffron is unobtainable, you can color the rice yellow with a pinch of turmeric powder.

Sambals
Curry dishes are frequently accompanied by 'cooling' garnishes, served as side dishes and known as 'sambals.' These include lemon wedges, tomato and onion slices, plain yogurt and pineapple chunks.

CHEF'S CHOICE
Seafish Stews

Fish stews are well loved by French and Italian cooks and on the following pages we show you how to make one of the most famous: Fisherman's Stew, or Matelote, as the French call it. Use our step-by-step guide to create this classic dish, and sample the true flavor of Mediterranean cooking. And try our two other special fish recipes: Eel Stew and Oslo Fish Stew — two vastly different dishes which prove just how versatile fish can be.

10

1 Wash the fish and cut them across the bone into thick slices **2** Place the fish in a flameproof casserole and add the sliced leek, celery, onion and shallots, the bouquet garni and the wine **3** Bring to a boil and simmer for 15-20 minutes **4** Heat butter in a skillet and add the diced bacon. Fry for 4 minutes. Lift out the bacon and keep warm **5** In the same fat, sauté the mushrooms for about 3 minutes. Drain and keep warm **6** In a separate pan, heat butter, add the pearl onions and sauté for 4-5 minutes until golden. Drain and keep warm **7** When the fish is cooked, lift out the pieces and place them in a serving dish **8** Add the bacon, mushrooms and onions. Keep the dish warm while thickening the stock **9** Strain the stock and bring it to a boil. Mix the butter with the flour to make a paste. Whisk the paste into the boiling stock, a little at a time, to make a thickened sauce. Check the seasoning and simmer the sauce for 5 minutes **10** Strain the sauce over the fish pieces. Dip the points of the fried bread shapes in the sauce and then in the chopped parsley and arrange them around the dish

Fisherman's Stew (Matelote)

4 lbs. varied white fish, cleaned
  and without heads
salt and pepper
1 leek (white part only), sliced
1 branch celery, sliced
1 onion, sliced
2 shallots, sliced
bouquet garni
1 bottle red wine
6 tablespoons butter
¼ lb. bacon, diced
½ lb. mushrooms, washed
  and trimmed
2 cups pearl onions, peeled
¼ cup flour

For the Garnish:
6 slices bread
½ cup oil
1 tablespoon chopped parsley

1 Wash the fish and cut them across the bone into thick slices. Place the fish pieces in a flame-proof casserole, season with salt and pepper, and add the sliced leek, celery, onion and shallots, the bouquet garni and the wine.

2 Place the dish over heat and bring to a boil. Reduce the heat and leave to simmer for 15-20 minutes.

3 Meanwhile, heat 2 tablespoons butter in a skillet, add the diced bacon and fry for about 4 minutes. Lift the bacon from the fat and keep warm.

4 To the same fat add the mushrooms and sauté them gently for 3 minutes. Drain and keep them warm.

5 In a separate pan, heat 2 tablespoons butter, add the pearl onions and sauté them for about 4-5 minutes until golden. Drain.

6 When the fish is cooked, lift out the fish pieces using a slotted spoon and place them in a serving dish. Add the drained bacon, mushrooms and pearl onions. Keep these ingredients warm while thickening the stock.

7 Strain the stock. Mix the remaining butter with the flour to make a paste. Bring the stock to a boil. Gradually whisk the butter and flour paste into the boiling stock, a little at a time, to form a sauce. Simmer for 5 minutes and check the seasoning.

8 Cut the slices of bread into heart shapes. Heat the oil in a skillet and fry the bread shapes for a few minutes, turning them until they are golden-brown on both sides. Drain.

9 Strain the thickened sauce over the fish pieces. Dip the points of the bread shapes in the sauce and then in the chopped parsley. Arrange the bread around the dish and serve.

Serves 6

Stewed Fish-balls
The flesh of any white fish can be ground with breadcrumbs, bound with beaten egg and shaped into fish balls. Stew the fish 'dumplings' with vegetables and serve with rice. Alternatively, cook the fish-balls in stock and serve them with a paprika or curry sauce. (See page 404 for the recipe for Fish-balls with Vegetables.)

Matelote Marinière
The Fisherman's Stew or Matelote recipe we have given here can be varied by using white wine instead of red — a dish which the French would term 'Matelote Marinière' and which would include mussels as a garnish.

Shellfish Sauces
The delicate flavor of white fish is well complemented by that of shellfish and so a shellfish sauce is the ideal accompaniment to plainly cooked white fish. Try Nantua, Shrimp or Cardinal Sauce; all three are basic béchamel sauces which are flavored with crayfish, shrimp and lobster, respectively.

Eel Stew

2 lbs. eel, cut across into 1¼-inch
  steaks
3 tablespoons flour
2 cups sliced onions
6 tablespoons butter
½ cup dry white wine
1 teaspoon tomato paste
pinch curry powder
pinch saffron
salt and pepper
3 tablespoons heavy cream
1 tablespoon chopped parsley
1 tablespoon chopped tarragon

1 Clean the eel steaks. Wash and drain them and dredge them in flour.

2 Melt 2 tablespoons butter in a pan. When it is hot, add the onions and sauté over low heat, stirring frequently. When they are just golden-brown, remove from the pan and set aside.

3 Melt the rest of the butter in the same pan and arrange the eel steaks side by side in the pan. Brown them well on both sides.

4 Mix the wine, tomato paste, curry powder and saffron. Season with salt and pepper and add this mixture to the pan, then arrange the onions around the slices of fish. Cover and simmer for 30 minutes.

5 Heat a serving dish.

6 Five minutes before serving, add the cream to the sauce, blending well. Shake the pan gently to achieve the best results. Test and correct seasoning.

7 Arrange the slices of eel in the heated dish. Sprinkle with the chopped herbs. Coat with the sauce and serve piping hot.

Serves 4

Oslo Fish Stew

¼ lb. cod fillet
6 potatoes, peeled and sliced
3 onions, peeled and cut in wedges
6 tomatoes, skinned, seeded and
  cut in wedges
2 sweet red peppers, seeded and
  cut in strips

1 cucumber, peeled and cut in
  thick chunks
2 cloves garlic, crushed (optional)
1 teaspoon salt
pinch black pepper
½ cup olive oil

1 Preheat the oven to 425°F. Cut the fish fillet across in thick slices.

2 Layer the fish and the vegetables in an ovenproof casserole. Season

Oslo Fish Stew — a tempting dish of cod, onions, tomatoes, peppers and garlic

and pour in the oil. Cover with a lid and place in the preheated oven for about 45 minutes or until the vegetables are cooked. Serve straight from the casserole.

Serves 4

Fish au Gratin

The term 'au gratin' means to form a thin crust on the top of certain dishes by browning in the oven or under the broiler.

Baked Tuna au Gratin

¼ cup butter
¼ cup flour
1¼ cups milk
2 egg yolks
1 cup grated cheese
salt and pepper
pinch grated nutmeg
1 lb. tuna, drained and
  flaked
2 cups cooked mashed potato

1 Preheat the oven to 400°F. Make the cheese sauce: melt 2 table-spoons of the butter in a pan, add the flour and cook the roux for 1 minute, without browning. Take the pan off the heat and gradually blend in the milk. Return to the heat and cook the sauce until thickened, stirring constantly. Remove from the heat and add 1 egg yolk and ½ cup of the grated cheese. Stir until well blended. Add salt and pepper to taste and the nutmeg.

2 Place the tuna in a shallow oven-proof dish, cover with the cheese sauce and sprinkle on the remaining grated cheese.

3 Blend the mashed potatoes with the remaining egg yolk and butter. Pass the potato through a strainer and then pipe it in an attractive pattern around the serving dish.

4 Place the dish in the preheated oven for about 12 minutes to brown the top. Serve with green beans or other green vegetables.

Serves 4

Cod Oriental

2 tablespoons butter
four 6-oz. cod fillets
salt and pepper
pinch paprika
1 teaspoon curry powder
1 onion, sliced
1 tablespoon shredded coconut
bouquet garni
1¼ cups water
juice 1 lemon
1 tablespoon tomato paste
⅔ cup plain yogurt
1½ tablespoons cornstarch
1 tablespoon oil
1 tablespoon chopped parsley

1 Preheat the oven to 400°F. Butter a shallow ovenproof dish and place the fish in it. Season and add paprika, curry powder, onion, shredded coconut and bouquet garni.

2 Mix the water, lemon juice and tomato paste and pour on the fish. Bake in the oven for 20 minutes.

3 Lift the fish from the sauce and keep warm. Strain the sauce into a pan and boil it for 10 minutes. Strain again and add the yogurt, cornstarch and oil. Check the seasoning.

4 Place the fish in a shallow dish and coat with the sauce. Sprinkle with the chopped parsley and serve.

Serves 4

Sole au Gratin

six 3-oz. sole fillets
¼ cup oil
2 tablespoons minced shallots
¼ cup chopped onion
½ lb. chopped mushrooms
2 cups fresh breadcrumbs
1 tablespoon tomato paste
1 beef bouillon cube
⅔ cup dry white wine
2 tablespoons butter
3 tablespoons grated Parmesan
1 tablespoon chopped parsley
½ lemon

1 Preheat the oven to 400°F. Clean the sole fillets if they aren't already. Heat the oil in a pan and add the chopped shallots and onions. Cook for about 5 minutes until soft and lightly browned. Add the mush-rooms and cook 5 minutes longer, until all the moisture has evapor-ated. Stir in the breadcrumbs.

2 Mix the tomato paste, crumbled beef bouillon cube and wine and add to the pan. Bring to a boil and cook for 5 minutes to form a sauce.

3 Roll the sole fillets loosely, place them on an ovenproof serving dish and cover with the sauce. Dot the butter on top and bake in the preheated oven for 15-20 minutes.

4 Remove from the oven and sprinkle the dish with the Parmesan and parsley. Return to the oven for 5 minutes to brown the top.

5 Serve with a squeeze of lemon.

Serves 6

Sole au Gratin. This delicious recipe brings out the delicate flavor of the sole

Fish 'n Rice

Salmon Kedgeree

1 cup heavy cream
2 large tomatoes, skinned, seeded and chopped
2 cups cooked long grain rice
1½ lbs. salmon, drained and flaked
2 tablespoons lemon juice
dash Tabasco sauce
1 teaspoon salt
½ cup grated Parmesan cheese
2 tablespoons butter

1 Preheat the oven to 400°F. Beat the cream until stiff.

2 Put all the ingredients, except the cheese and butter, in a bowl, then fold gently to combine.

3 Transfer the mixture to a buttered baking dish, sprinkle with the cheese, then dot with the butter. Bake in the preheated oven for 15-20 minutes until hot and bubbling. Serve immediately.

Serves 6

Look 'n Cook Cuts of Fresh Fish

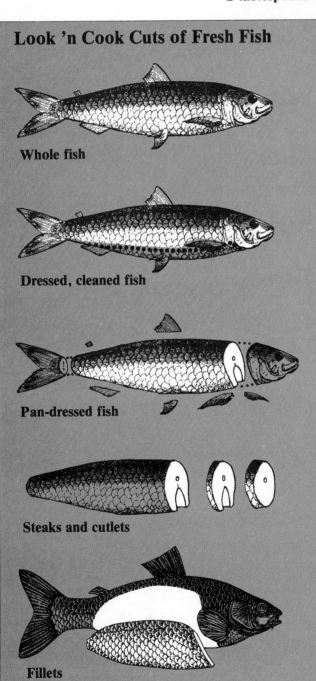

Whole fish

Dressed, cleaned fish

Pan-dressed fish

Steaks and cutlets

Fillets

Whole fish are sold exactly as they are caught, so before cooking, the fins, scales, gills and entrails must be removed. Whether the head and tail are left on is a matter of choice. Some small fish are cooked whole with only the entrails removed. Allow 1 lb. per serving.

Dressed or cleaned fish are sold with the entrails and gills removed. Cut off the fins and, to remove the scales, grip the tail and scrape from the tail to the head, with the knife at an angle. The head and tail may be left on, if preferred. Allow 1 lb. per serving

Pan-dressed fish, as they are sometimes called, are those bought ready to cook, that is the head, tail, fins, entrails, gills and scales have all been removed. Large fish may be cut into smaller portions of 1- or 2-lb. weight. Allow ½ lb. per serving.

Steaks and cutlets are thick slices of large fish, cut through the backbone; steaks are from the tail end and cutlets from the middle of the fish. The skin is left on, but the central bone can be removed before cooking and the cavity filled with stuffing. Allow 1 lb. for 2-3 servings.

Fillets are the side sections of the fish cut along the length of the body. They can be taken from both round and flat fish and are very popular cuts because the solid pieces of fish contain very few bones. The skin is also often removed. Allow 1 lb. for 3 servings.

Frozen fish, if correctly processed, retains all the flavor of fresh fish and the two are interchangeable. Whole large fish, like salmon, must be slowly and thoroughly defrosted in the refrigerator and then cooked as soon as they are thawed. Cutlets, steaks, fillets and small whole fish, like trout, however, can be cooked from frozen. Remember, though, that once thawed, raw fish must never be frozen again unless cooked first.

Seafood Salad

2 tablespoons oil
1 small onion, chopped
$\frac{7}{8}$ cup long grain rice
2$\frac{1}{4}$ cups fish stock, or water with 1 chicken bouillon cube added
2 ozs. anchovy fillets, drained
$\frac{1}{3}$ cup olive oil
2 tablespoons lemon juice
1 teaspoon anchovy paste
pinch freshly ground black pepper
1 lb. cooked, peeled, deveined shrimp

2$\frac{1}{4}$ cups cooked peas
9 ozs. mussels
pinch finely chopped dill

1 Heat the oil in a pan, add the onion and sauté for 3-4 minutes. Add the rice and sauté for a further 1-2 minutes. Pour on the fish stock, or the water and bouillon cube, cover and let the rice cook for about 25 minutes or until the liquid has been absorbed. When cooked, transfer to a serving dish.

2 Mash the anchovy fillets and mix them with the salad oil, lemon juice, anchovy paste and pepper.

Seafood Salad—shrimp, mussels, anchovies and rice make a tasty chilled dish.

Pour this mixture onto the cooked rice and allow to cool. Place in the refrigerator to chill completely.

3 When ready to serve, add the shrimp, peas and mussels and sprinkle with the dill. Serve with toast for supper or as an appetizer.

Serves 4

415

Molded Cod and Shrimp in Aspic

¼ cup short grain rice
1¼ cups fish stock
1 egg yolk
⅔ cup flaked, cooked cod
¼ lb. cooked, peeled, deveined
  shrimp
pinch nutmeg
salt and pepper
1 cup chicken stock, or water with
  1 chicken bouillon cube added
¼ cup gelatin

For the Garnish:
cucumber and lemon slices

1 Put the short grain rice and fish stock in a pan, bring to a boil and simmer for 10 minutes.

2 Add the egg yolk, flaked cod, shrimp, nutmeg and salt and pepper and blend well.

3 Put the chicken stock, or water and bouillon cube, in a pan and bring to a boil. Take off the heat, add the gelatin and stir until dissolved. Cool.

4 Pour half the dissolved gelatin in an 8-inch ring mold, place the mold in a bowl of ice and tilt it so that the gelatin coats the sides and base of the mold as it cools.

5 Add the rest of the dissolved gelatin to the fish mixture and blend well. Pour into the mold and leave in the refrigerator for 1 hour to set.

6 Invert the mold onto a serving dish and decorate with cucumber and lemon slices.

Serves 6

Tip: Tarragon leaves may also be used to decorate the ring, in which case add 1 teaspoon tarragon vinegar to the fish mixture before chilling.

Molded Cod and Shrimp in Aspic — a perfect picnic treat which can be prepared in advance

Broiled Fish

Broiling is one of the best methods of cooking fish. It is especially suited to oily fish: herring, mackerel, sardines, trout, salmon, shad and others. When broiling a whole, round fish, first clean it, if necessary (the fish dealer will usually do this for you), then scale, wash and dry. If you like, the head and tail can be removed, although it is usual to leave them on both broiled and fried fish. The practice of cutting the tail into a deep V-shape is known as 'Vandyking.' Score the fish on both sides by making 2-3 diagonal cuts with a knife: this helps it to cook evenly, without burning the outside and leaving the inside half-raw. Brush it with oil or clarified butter, sprinkle with salt, a little prepared mustard or lemon juice — or top with a delicious savory butter. Line the broiler with foil so that the fishy smell doesn't linger in your kitchen after cooking. Broil at a high temperature, turning the fish once, carefully, and brushing the second side with oil. Allow 8 minutes to cook a fish 1 inch thick. For a special decorative touch, heat a skewer in an open flame till red-hot; then mark the fish with a criss-cross pattern just before serving. Serve broiled fish with a piquant sauce — the sharpness takes the edge off the richness of the fish — or one with a garlic or herb base, or topped with pats of savory butter, and accompany with plain boiled potatoes or rice.

White fish is also excellent broiled, especially if it has been lightly marinated first to bring out its flavor. Steep it in a mixture of oil, lemon juice or wine vinegar, seasoned with salt and pepper. Add crushed garlic, a little sugar, soy sauce, sliced onion, a pinch of cayenne and fresh herbs such as tarragon, fennel or thyme: the combinations are endless.

Broiled fish is rich in protein and vitamins, and is a vital part of a calorie-controlled, low fat diet. Serving fish as kebabs or with an oriental sauce is an original variation on plain broiled fish, and both make excellent party dishes.

Baltic Cod Kebabs

14 ozs. cod fingers or fillets
4 pearl onions
4 firm tomatoes, skinned and halved
4 mushrooms, washed
1 teaspoon chopped dill
1 sprig parsley
1 lemon, cut in wedges
For the Marinade:
⅓ cup olive oil
juice 1 lemon
2 teaspoons Worcestershire sauce
salt and pepper

1 Cut the fish into 1-inch cubes and place in a bowl.

2 Mix the marinade ingredients together and pour over the cubes of cod. Soak in the marinade for 30 minutes.

3 Parboil the pearl onions for 5 minutes.

4 Skewer the cod cubes, tomatoes, mushrooms and onions on four long, metal skewers. Brush with the remaining marinade and season.

5 Place under a broiler or over a grill or barbecue for 8-10 minutes. Brush with oil or melted butter from time to time.

6 Sprinkle the cooked kebabs with chopped dill and garnish with parsley and lemon wedges. Serve with tartar sauce and plain boiled rice.

Serves 4

Baltic Cod Kebabs — marinated pieces of cod threaded on skewers with mushrooms, onions and tomatoes and broiled or barbecued

1 Ingredients: large white fish, mackerel, red mullet, salmon, sardines, sole, lemon and thyme **2** Place the large white fish in a shallow dish, baste with oil and cover with crushed bay leaf, thyme and lemon slices **3** Place under a broiler **4** When the fish is cooked on one side, turn it over and broil the other **5** and **6** Repeat the same procedure when broiling salmon **7** Arrange mackerel and red mullet under a broiler and lightly salt **8** Turn the mackerel over to cook the other side and salt again **9** Dip the sole in oil and then flour both sides **10** Place the sole under a hot broiler and cook on one side, then the other. You can make a criss-cross pattern on the fish with a red-hot skewer **11** Garnish broiled fish with chopped parsley, lemon quarters or slices

Broiled Mackerel Fillets with Berry Sauce

eight ½-lb. mackerel or shad fillets, washed
¼ cup flour
salt and pepper
pinch paprika
¼ cup oil

For the Marinade:
3 tablespoons oil
grated rind and juice 1 lemon
1 tablespoon soy sauce
1 clove garlic, peeled and crushed
1 tablespoon wine vinegar
1 tablespoon sugar

For the Berry Sauce:
½ lb. berries, trimmed
1 apple, peeled, cored and diced
¼ cup sugar
sprig mint
⅔ cup water
1 tablespoon cornstarch (optional)

1 Blend all the ingredients for the marinade in a blender.

2 Soak the fish fillets in the marinade for 15 minutes. Drain them and dry on absorbent paper, then dip in seasoned flour.

3 Brush the fillets with oil and place on a greased broiler rack. Broil for 3 minutes on each side, then remove, season with salt and pepper, and arrange on a hot dish. Keep warm.

4 Place the berries in a saucepan with the diced apple, sugar, mint and half of the water. Boil for 8 minutes, then discard the mint.

5 Work the berry mixture in a blender or through a food mill to a purée. Add a pinch of salt. Heat the purée in a small saucepan and thicken, if liked, with the cornstarch mixed to a paste with the rest of the water. Boil for 4 minutes until clear and thick.

6 Serve the grilled mackerel with the berry sauce.

Serves 4

Broiled Herring with Bacon

1¼ cups milk
¼ cup butter
¼ cup flour
pinch grated nutmeg
salt and pepper
four ½-lb. herring
4 slices bacon
bunch parsley
2 hard-boiled eggs
1½ lemons

1 Preheat the broiler.

2 Heat the milk in a small saucepan for the white sauce.

3 Melt 2 tablespoons butter, stir in the flour and cook for 2 minutes.

4 Add the hot milk to the roux, little by little, stirring all the time until the sauce is very smooth. Add the grated nutmeg, salt and pepper. Cook over low heat with the lid on.

5 Melt the remaining butter and baste the herring. Place under the broiler for 10-12 minutes. Turn the fish over when cooked on one side.

6 Broil the bacon slices at the same time.

7 Meanwhile, wash and dry the parsley. Mince half the bunch finely, and reserve. Add the other half to the sauce, tied with string around the stems.

8 Shell the hard-boiled eggs, and mash with a fork in a bowl. Squeeze on the half lemon.

9 Remove the parsley from the sauce, and stir in the mashed eggs and lemon juice. Mix well, season with salt and pepper, pour into a sauce boat and keep hot.

10 Arrange the herring on a warm serving dish, and place one slice of warm, broiled bacon on each. Garnish with lemon slices and parsley. Serve immediately with the hot sauce.

Serves 4

Broiled Arabian Bass

3-lb. bass or any large fish
2 tablespoons oil
1 tablespoon cumin
salt and pepper

For the Sauce:
2½ cups water
3 tablespoons oil
4 onions, sliced
1 tablespoon paprika
¼ cup tomato paste
small bunch celery leaves, washed and dried
2 cloves garlic, crushed
juice 1 lemon

1 Carefully scrape the scales off the bass, as its skin is delicate, and clean, wash and dry it. Make two light slashes across the skin crossways. Baste the bass with oil and sprinkle inside and out with half of the cumin, salt and pepper.

2 Broil the bass under low heat, turning it frequently and basting. Meanwhile, make the sauce.

3 Boil the water in a saucepan. Heat the oil in a sauté pan and add the onions. Stir in the paprika, tomato paste, the rest of the cumin, celery leaves and garlic.

4 Pour the mixture into the boiling water. Add the lemon juice, salt and pepper, and boil until the liquid has reduced by half.

5 Arrange the cooked bass on a heated serving dish and garnish with lemon quarters.

6 Remove the celery leaves from the sauce and adjust the seasoning. Serve very hot in a sauce boat.

Serves 4

Broiled Herring with Bacon would make a delicious meal at suppertime

Broiled Bass with Fennel

2-lb. bass
salt and pepper
7 sprigs fennel
$\frac{1}{4}$ lb. butter, softened
$\frac{1}{4}$ cup oil
1 lemon

1 Wash and clean the bass.

2 Make several criss-cross cuts on both sides of the fish. Sprinkle with salt and pepper and place 2 sprigs of fennel and 1 tablespoon butter inside the bass.

3 Baste the bass with the oil and place under a hot broiler for 40 minutes, turning and basting occasionally, and adjusting the heat as necessary.

4 Crush 3 sprigs of fennel with a pestle in a mortar. Blend with the remaining butter in a cup. Place in refrigerator until chilled but still pliable; then roll the butter in aluminum foil into a cylindrical shape. Replace in the refrigerator.

5 Chop the remaining 2 sprigs of fennel, and sprinkle over the cooked bass. Take the fennel butter from the refrigerator, and slice into thin rounds. Allow the bass to cook for 30 seconds more.

6 Place the bass on a heated serving dish, and serve with wedges of lemon and the slices of chilled fennel butter.

Serves 4

Tip: Use dried fennel or oregano, or sprigs of fresh marjoram if fresh fennel is not available.

Broiled Flounder with Anchovy Butter

four $\frac{1}{2}$-lb. flounder or sole
3 lemons
$1\frac{1}{4}$ cups oil
1 tablespoon thyme
$\frac{1}{2}$ bay leaf, crushed
1 bunch parsley
1 cup flour
salt and pepper

For the Anchovy Butter:
$\frac{1}{4}$ cup canned anchovy fillets, drained
$\frac{1}{4}$ lb. butter

Broiled Bass with Fennel. This fragrant herb is used to flavor both the fish and the accompanying savory butter

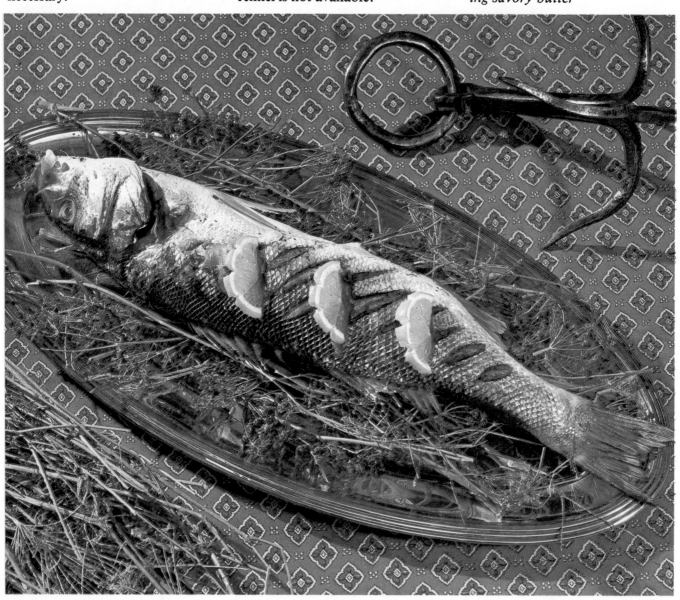

1 Remove the skin from the fish. Score the white skin with a knife and make a small incision in the side of each fish. Clean and wash the fish.

2 Peel one of the lemons, removing all the pith. Slice thinly and place the slices in a deep bowl. Pour in the oil and sprinkle with the thyme and crushed bay leaf.

3 Soak the anchovies in cold water to remove excess salt.

4 Pound the butter and anchovies until they are blended together and the mixture is smooth. Roll in foil to make a cylinder shape and chill in the refrigerator. Cut into slices.

5 Coat the fish with the flour and dip into the oil and lemon mixture. Drain and season.

6 Place under a hot broiler, white side down. When the first side is cooked, turn the fish carefully and brown the second side.

7 While the fish are cooking, cut the 2 remaining lemons into quarters.

8 Arrange the fish on a heated serving dish. Garnish with the parsley, and serve with the anchovy butter.

Serves 4

Nut Butter

¼ lb. chopped nuts (any one or a
  mixture of chopped hazelnuts,
  peanuts, walnuts, almonds and
  shredded coconut)
scant ⅔ cup butter

1 Preheat the oven to 400°F. Spread the chopped nuts and/or shredded coconut on a roasting pan and toast in the preheated oven for 5 minutes until browned. Remove from the oven and allow to cool.

2 Pound the nuts with the butter to produce a paste.

Use with broiled fish

Mustard Butter

¼ lb. butter, softened
1-2 tablespoons prepared French
  (Dijon-style) mustard
salt and pepper

1 Cream the butter in a bowl.

2 Beat in the mustard and salt and pepper to taste and keep in a cool

Savory Butters — softened butter blended with a flavoring and chilled in the refrigerator — make excellent garnishes for broiled fish

place until required. Place a pat on each portion of meat or fish just before serving.

Serve with broiled fish

Tip: Vary the flavor by using different kinds of mustard.

Skillet-fried Fish

Fish, skillet-fried, should be tasty, crisp and fresh. All kinds of fish lend themselves to this method of cooking, from herring or trout to fillets of flounder or sole; and cod or haddock steaks. First clean and dry the fish, scaling and gutting if necessary. Then coat it in seasoned flour, or matzo or corn meal. (This seals in its flavor, and prevents it from sticking to the pan.) Make sure the fish is evenly coated — shake off excess flour. Heat a heavy frying pan or skillet and pour in enough oil to reach a depth of about $\frac{1}{4}$ inch. When the oil is very hot, place the fish in it and fry it quickly, turning it once, for 2 minutes. Lower the heat, and let it cook thoroughly. Drain and dry on absorbent paper. Serve immediately, with a tangy tartar sauce, French fries or creamed potatoes, seasonal vegetables, and a generous wedge of lemon.

You may fry in cooking fats

Trout with Almonds. Coat the fish with seasoned flour and skillet-fry. Then sprinkle with lightly-toasted, sliced almonds and serve garnished with lemon slices

(shortening) or use a mixture of oil and clarified butter. Fish dipped in beaten egg, then rolled in fine breadcrumbs or oatmeal (after being ground) is especially delicious fried. Fried fish is a perennial family favorite — but when it is cooked à la Meunière, it becomes a classic of French cuisine. Coat the fish evenly with seasoned flour, then cook it gently in clarified butter whch is hot, but not brown. (Add a little oil.) When it is ready, keep the fish hot, squeeze the juice of $\frac{1}{2}$ lemon over it, and sprinkle with chopped parsley. Melt a little butter until it is frothy and lightly colored and pour it on the fish. Fish Meunière can be adapted to a range of recipes, and each different garnish — like tomatoes, capers, or shrimp and mushrooms — has its own title in classic French cookery.

Fried Herring

bunch parsley
2 lemons
⅔ cup butter
salt and pepper
four ½-lb. fresh herring, cleaned,
  boned and split in two
6 slices dry bread
1 egg, beaten
¼ cup flour
2 tablespoons oil

1 Wash, dry and finely chop half the parsley. Squeeze 1 lemon.

2 Slightly warm a bowl. Put in ½ cup butter and soften it with a wooden spoon. Mix in the lemon juice, the chopped parsley and some salt and pepper. Form a roll with this butter. Put on a small dish and chill in the refrigerator to harden it.

3 Wash the fish pieces and dry them. Crumble the bread.

4 Pour the beaten egg onto a plate, put the breadcrumbs on another and the flour on a third.

5 Melt the rest of the butter and the oil in a skillet.

6 Dip the fillets into the flour, then into the egg and then into the breadcrumbs. Press the breadcrumbs to the fish with the blade of a knife. Put the fillets into the hot butter and oil and cook for 4 minutes on each side over low heat, turning with a large spatula.

7 Flute the skin of the other lemon with a zesting knife. Cut the lemon into slices. Heat a serving dish.

8 When the fillets are cooked, arrange on the dish. Surround them with the slices of lemon and the rest of the parsley. Serve hot with the parsley butter.

Serves 4

Tip: To complement the parsley butter, you can serve a parsley sauce, made either from your favorite recipe or using a packaged mix.

Herrings Fried in Oatmeal

4 fresh herring, cleaned
½ cup milk
½ cup oatmeal
1 teaspoon salt
freshly ground black pepper
3 tablespoons butter

For the Mustard Sauce:
2 tablespoons butter
2 tablespoons flour
1¼ cups milk
2 teaspoons Dijon-style
  mustard
1 teaspoon lemon juice

1 Rinse and dry the fish. Dip them first in the milk and then in the oatmeal, pressing the oatmeal onto

Fried Herring, garnished with lemon slices and parsley and accompanied by parsley sauce

the fish with a broad-bladed knife. Season.

2 Melt the butter in a large skillet. Fry the herring for 5 minutes on each side over moderate heat.

3 Meanwhile, make the sauce. Melt the butter in a pan and stir in the flour. Cook the roux for 1 minute and then gradually blend in the milk. Bring to a boil and cook until thickened. Beat in the mustard, lemon juice and salt and pepper to taste.

4 Arrange the cooked herring on a heated serving dish. Serve hot with the mustard sauce.

Serves 4

Look 'n Cook Egging and Crumbing Fish for Frying

1 Ingredients: whiting (or cod), sole, oil, flour, eggs, bread, parsley, lemon, salt and pepper **2** To make Rolled Whiting: remove the backbone and skin and flour the whiting **3** and **4** Dip the fish in beaten egg and then coat in breadcrumbs **5** Press down with the flat side of a knife to make the breadcrumbs stick to it **6** Roll up the two fillets, one on each side of the head, and hold in place with a metal skewer **7** To make fish fillets: prepare the fish in the same way and make a criss-cross pattern on each fillet with a knife **8** To make Sole Goujons: cut the fillets into fine strips **9** Coat the strips with egg and breadcrumbs **10** The fish ready for frying

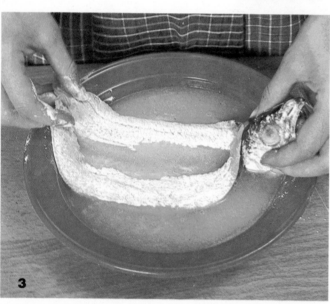

7

8

9

10

Sautéed Salmon with Creamed Mushrooms

2 tablespoons butter
¾ cup flour
⅓ cup water
⅔ cup light cream
salt and pepper
1-2 tablespoons dry sherry
½ lb. mushrooms, cut in
 quarters, and sautéed in butter
6 salmon steaks, ½ lb. each
½ cup oil
1 lemon
lettuce leaves

1 Melt the butter in a pan, add 4 tablespoons flour and cook the roux for 1 minute. Take the pan off the heat and blend in the reserved liquid from the mushrooms, the water and the cream. Cook the sauce for 5 minutes without boiling, add salt and pepper and the sherry and simmer for a further 10 minutes. Add the mushrooms and heat for 3 minutes more.

2 Season the rest of the flour and dust the salmon steaks with the flour.

3 Heat the oil in a pan, add the steaks and sauté for 4-5 minutes on each side until golden-brown. Place the steaks on a serving dish and spoon a little of the sauce on each one. Garnish with the lemon, cut into an attractive shape, and the lettuce leaves.

Serves 6

Sautéed Salmon with Creamed Mushrooms. The mushroom, sherry and cream sauce complements the flavor of the salmon

Flounder Fillets with Shrimp

2 tablespoons flour
½ cup breadcrumbs
salt
2 eggs, well beaten
4 fillets of flounder
2 tablespoons oil
⅔ cup butter
½ lb. cooked, peeled, deveined
 shrimp
1 lemon

1 Put the flour on one plate and the breadcrumbs on another. Add salt to the eggs.

2 Salt the fillets of flounder, and dip them, on both sides, into the flour. Shake them gently to get rid of the excess flour, then dip them into the beaten egg, and lastly into the breadcrumbs. Press the breadcrumbs firmly onto the fish.

3 Put the fillets on a plate and place in the refrigerator for 10 minutes.

4 Heat the oil and 3 tablespoons butter in a skillet and sauté the fillets of fish for 2 or 3 minutes on each side, turning them carefully with a spatula.

5 Remove from the skillet and arrange them on a heated serving dish. Keep hot.

6 Melt 3 tablespoons butter over low heat in a small saucepan. Pour in the shrimp and shake the pan until all are coated with butter (2 or 3 minutes).

7 Arrange a row of shrimp down the middle of each fillet and keep hot.

8 Heat the rest of the butter in the same saucepan until it is a nutty brown, and pour this over the fish fillets.

9 Cut the lemon into quarters. Garnish the dish with the lemon quarters and serve very hot.

Serves 4

Flounder Fillets with Shrimp — deep-fried flounder decorated with shrimp tossed in melted butter

Look 'n Cook Trout Meunière

1 Heat a mixture of butter and oil in a large, oval skillet and, when foaming, add the floured trout. Arrange side by side and cook gently on one side **2** Turn the trout over and cook the other side **3** Arrange the cooked trout on a warm serving dish and sprinkle with chopped parsley **4** Heat the remainder of the butter in a pan until frothing and pour over the trout **5** Garnish the dish with peeled lemon slices and more chopped parsley. Serve with sautéed mushrooms

Trout Meunière

four ½-lb. trout
salt and pepper
½ cup flour
⅔ cup butter
¼ cup oil
2 lemons
1 tablespoon chopped parsley

1 Wash and dry the trout and season with salt and pepper.

2 Roll the trout in flour and shake off the excess.

3 Heat 4 tablespoons butter and the oil in a large, oval skillet. When foaming, add the trout and cook gently on both sides.

4 Meanwhile, cut vertical grooves in the skin of a lemon and slice thinly. Peel another lemon and cut into slices.

5 Arrange the cooked trout on a buttered serving dish and sprinkle with the chopped parsley. Keep hot.

6 Heat the remainder of the butter in a pan until it is frothing and pour over the trout. Garnish with the lemon slices.

Serves 4

Tip: Sole or flounder can be used as a substitute for trout. Use the fish whole and do not remove the white skin or cut off the fillets. Cook in the same manner as for trout.

Variations

Belle Meunière: Garnish the trout with peeled, seeded tomatoes and sautéed mushrooms.

Bretonne: Garnish the trout with peeled shrimp and sliced sautéed mushrooms.

Doria: Decorate the trout with chopped, sautéed cucumber.

Marseillaise: Garnish with sautéed eggplants, tomatoes and garlic butter.

Flounder in Black Butter

2 lbs. flounder
¼ lb. butter
2 tablespoons vinegar
2 tablespoons capers
1 tablespoon chopped parsley

For the Stock:
2¼ cups water
⅓ cup vinegar
1 onion, chopped
1 carrot, chopped
bouquet garni
salt and pepper

1 Cut the flounder into equal-size pieces.

2 Put all the ingredients for the stock in a large pan and boil for 10 minutes (until the onion and carrot are soft).

3 Add the fish and poach for 5-6 minutes. Remove the flounder, drain well and place in a serving dish. Keep hot.

4 Heat the butter in a skillet until it is brown and foaming — almost black. Add the vinegar immediately and pour on the fish.

5 Sprinkle with capers and chopped parsley and serve.

Serves 4

Skillet-fried Mullet

four ½-lb. red mullet
2 tablespoons seasoned flour
¼ cup oil
¼ lb. butter
4 bananas
2 ears of fresh corn
2 tablespoons chopped parsley

1 Clean and wash the mullet and turn in seasoned flour.

2 Heat the oil and 4 tablespoons butter in a skillet and cook the mullet gently on both sides until cooked. Arrange in a serving dish and keep hot.

3 Split the bananas in two and heat the remainder of the butter in a pan. Fry the bananas until soft.

4 Place the corn in a saucepan and cover with water. Boil for 5-8 minutes, slice into 8 pieces and season.

5 Sprinkle the mullet with chopped parsley and serve with the corn slices and fried bananas.

Serves 4

Sole Murat

This famous recipe was created by M. Dinan who was chef to Marshall Murat and later to Napoleon when he was imprisoned on St. Helena.

¾ lb. fillets of sole
¼ cup flour
3 medium-size potatoes, boiled
½ lb. artichoke hearts
¼ cup butter
¼ cup oil
salt and pepper
juice 1 lemon
1 tablespoon chopped parsley

1 Cut the fillets into strips ¼ inch wide by 2 inches long and dredge with flour.

2 Cut the potatoes and artichokes into strips — the same size as the sole strips.

3 Heat the butter and oil in a skillet and sauté the strips of sole, potatoes and artichokes for 8-10 minutes. Cover the pan with a lid and toss from time to time. Season with salt and pepper.

4 Arrange the sautéed strips in a serving dish and sprinkle with lemon juice and chopped parsley.

Serves 4

Skillet-fried Haddock

2 lbs. haddock
salt and pepper
1 cup flour
1 egg, beaten
⅔ cup oil
4 cups fresh white breadcrumbs
3 tablespoons butter
2 lemons

1 Fillet the fish and wash and dry the fillets. Remove the skin and sprinkle fillets with salt and pepper.

2 Coat the fish fillets in the flour.

3 Blend the beaten egg with 1 tablespoon oil. Dip the fish fillets into this mixture and then coat with the breadcrumbs. Decorate the fillets by making a criss-cross pattern on both sides with a knife.

4 Heat the butter and remaining oil in a skillet. Add the fish and fry gently for 2-3 minutes on each side until lightly browned. Drain on absorbent paper.

5 Arrange the fish on a warm serving dish and decorate with lemon halves and slices. Serve with parsley butter.

Serves 4

Tip: Sole, red mullet or cod can be substituted for haddock in this recipe.

Zesting Lemons

This is best done with a special knife known as a 'lemon zester' or 'cannelle knife'. Draw the knife lengthwise (vertically) along the lemon at regular intervals all the way around. Then thinly slice the lemon across. Use as a garnish for decorating broiled and fried fish.

Garnishing and Presentation of Fried Fish

The following garnishes can be used to decorate most fried, coated fish such as sole, lemon sole, flounder or any flat fish.

Sauce Hollandaise
Pour a generous portion of hollandaise sauce onto each fried fish fillet and garnish with onion rings and chopped chives.

Shrimp in Hot Sauce
Sauté 1 chopped onion in 4 tablespoons butter and oil. Add a few capers and 3 tablespoons brandy. Stir in ¼ cup tomato paste, 2 drops Tabasco sauce and ½ cup heavy cream. Season and add ½ lb. peeled, deveined shrimp and boil for 5 minutes. Heap a spoonful of sauce onto each fish fillet and garnish with peeled shrimp.

Fish Roe and Mushrooms
Blend ¼ lb. sautéed, chopped mushrooms with 2 tablespoons heavy cream and ¼ lb. fish roe. Spread this mixture onto a fish fillet and top with another fillet. Fry until golden-brown and garnish with lemon and tomato slices.

Creamed Mussels
Stir ¼ lb. canned or fresh mussels into 1¼ cups velouté sauce. Heat through and season with salt and pepper. Place a spoonful on each fish fillet.

Tartar Sauce
Mix 1¼ cups mayonnaise with 2 teaspoons prepared French (Dijonstyle) mustard and 2 tablespoons chopped parsley, a pinch of chervil and tarragon and 1 tablespoon chopped, pickled cucumber. Stir in ¼ cup whipped cream. Place a spoonful of sauce on each fish fillet and garnish with shrimp, asparagus tips and lemon slices.

Green (Venetian) Butter

½ lb. spinach leaves
⅔ cup mixture tarragon and
   watercress
1 oz. canned anchovy fillets,
   drained
½ lb. butter, softened
pinch salt
pinch pepper
pinch nutmeg

1 Add the spinach, tarragon and watercress to a pan of boiling water and parboil for 5 minutes. Drain and squeeze out the moisture from the leaves. Work in a blender or through a food mill with the anchovy fillets to obtain a smooth purée. Allow the purée to cool.

2 Beat the butter in a bowl until softened and of a creamy consistency.

3 When the purée is cold, add it to the softened butter and mix until evenly blended. Season with salt, pepper and nutmeg.

Use with any broiled fish

Five Garnishes for fish fried in breadcrumbs — see recipes at left

Ravigote Butter

Use the same recipe as for the Green Butter, but add ½ cup minced shallots blanched in ½ cup dry white wine to the lettuce and herb leaves before blending.

Use with broiled fish

433

Deep-fried Fish

Deep-fried fish, coated with crisp batter or egg and breadcrumbs and served piping hot, is an irresistible family dish. Deep-frying is a good way of cooking white and oily fish, either whole, if small, or as fillets, strips, fish-balls and made-up mixtures like croquettes, patties and fish cakes.

You need a deep-fat fryer with a basket inside to hold the fish. You may use any vegetable oil or solid cooking shortening, but do not mix the two. Never fill the pan more than half-full of oil or fat, as it can very easily splatter. Make sure the cooking fat is completely clean.

To prepare fish for frying

1 Egg and crumb method: (see pages 426-427) wash and dry the fish completely — hot fat and water do not mix and splattering will occur. Dust the fish evenly with flour (shake off the excess) and dip it first in beaten egg, then in fine breadcrumbs (they can be white or brown).

2 Batter method: coat the floured fish in a savory batter (see page 438) seasoned to your taste.

Heat the oil or fat to 375°F. — check with a frying thermometer or by putting in a cube of bread which should turn brown within 1 minute and the oil or fat bubble around it as soon as it is submerged. Dip the basket into the hot fat or oil (this prevents food sticking to it), then lower the fish into the fryer. Fillets take 3-4 minutes to cook; thicker fish 5-6 minutes. When the fish is crisp and golden, take it out carefully, drain and dry thoroughly on absorbent paper. Serve immediately.

Never overfill the frying basket, as too much food causes a reduction in temperature, resulting in soggy or undercooked food. And *never* leave the fryer over heat unattended. Make sure the handle is turned inward and away from you, so there is no danger of knocking it over.

Deep-frying is a particularly tasty way of cooking white fish such as haddock or cod.

Fried White Fish

oil for deep frying
four ½-lb. fillets of white fish
1 cup beer
3 tablespoons flour
bunch parsley
2 lemons
salt

1 Heat the oil to 375°F.

2 Clean the fish fillets. Wash and dry them. Put them into a dish and cover with beer.

3 Pour the flour onto a plate, dip the drained fish into it and shake to remove excess flour.

4 Dip the basket into the hot oil and then lower the fish into the basket. Leave until the fish are cooked through and browned (about 4-5 minutes).

5 Wash and dry the parsley and untie the bunch.

6 Wash and dry the lemons. Cut into halves, serrating the edges. Heat a serving dish.

7 When the fish are cooked, drain them and place on a serving dish. Salt them, then arrange the half lemons around the dish.

8 Lower the parsley into the oil. Leave for about 2 seconds, then drain it. Decorate the plate with the fried parsley.

9 Serve very hot.

Serves 4

Tip: The oil should be very hot, but not boiling. Serve with fluffy mashed potatoes.

Fried Sardines (or Smelts)

16 large fresh sardines (or smelts)
handful sea salt
1 tablespoon dry breadcrumbs
1 tablespoon light cream
1 egg, separated
1 clove garlic, chopped
2 shallots, chopped
1 tablespoon chopped chives
1 tablespoon chopped chervil
salt and pepper
1¼ cups flour

oil for deep frying
1¼ cups milk
bunch parsley

1 Wash and dry the sardines. Place them in an earthenware dish. Sprinkle with the sea salt. Leave them for 4 hours in a cool place.

2 Mix the breadcrumbs and cream in a bowl. Add the egg yolk and mix again.

3 Add the garlic, shallots, chives and chervil to the cream and breadcrumbs. Add salt and pepper. Mix thoroughly with a wooden spoon.

4 Pour the flour onto a plate. Heat the oil to 375°F.

5 Clean the sardines if necessary. Gut them, cut out the backbone and fill with the cream stuffing. Reshape and secure the sardines with a wooden toothpick.

6 Put the stuffed sardines back into the earthenware dish, cover with the milk. Then dry them and dip into the flour one by one. Put them into the frying basket. Gently shake the basket to remove excess flour.

7 Lower the basket into the hot oil and fry until brown.

8 Heat a serving dish. Wash the parsley, dry well.

9 When the fish have browned, drain them and arrange on the serving dish.

10 Lower the parsley into the oil. Fry for 2 minutes, then drain it and arrange with the fish.

11 Serve very hot.

Serves 4

Deep-Fried Sole or Flounder with Zucchini Fritters

1¼ cups flour

2 eggs
1⅔ cups milk
1 tablespoon chopped parsley
1 garlic clove, peeled and crushed
salt and pepper
oil for deep frying
2 large zucchini, thinly sliced
four ½-lb. sole or flounder fillets
2 lemons

1 Preheat the oven to 275°F.

2 Prepare the batter for the zucchini. Sift ¾ cup of the flour into a bowl. Add the eggs and mix well together. Gradually stir in ⅞ cup of the milk. Add the chopped parsley, garlic and salt and pepper to taste. Mix well.

3 Half fill a deep fat fryer with oil and heat to 375°F.

4 Dip zucchini slices in flour, then coat with batter and lower into the oil. Cook for 3-4 minutes.

5 When the fritters are well browned, take them out of the oil, drain them on absorbent paper, put them into a heated vegetable dish, and keep them warm in the oven.

6 Rinse and dry the fish fillets. Pour the rest of the milk into a bowl. Spread the rest of the flour on a plate.

7 Dip the fillets into the milk, then coat them in the flour. Shake to remove excess flour. Dip the basket in the hot oil and then lower the fish into the basket and cook until brown on both sides.

8 Cut the lemons into halves (with a zig-zag edge, if liked).

9 Drain the fillets and arrange them on a white napkin on a heated serving dish. Place a lemon half on each fillet. Serve very hot with the zucchini fritters.

Serves 4

Tip: The fritter batter should be a lot thicker than pancake batter, so add a little extra flour if necessary.

Fish Tempura

Tempura is the Japanese name for a dish of lightly-fried pieces of meat, fish, poultry or vegetables, served straight from the pan with a soy sauce dip or raw vegetable salad.

2 lbs. fish fillets (e.g. haddock, mullet, cod, halibut)
juice 1 lemon
½ cup seasoned flour
oil for deep frying

For the Batter:
⅔ cup water
1 egg, beaten
1 tablespoon oil
¾ cup flour
pinch salt and pepper

1 Mix all the ingredients for the batter in a bowl.

2 Cut the fish fillets into small squares, cubes or strips. Sprinkle with the lemon juice and coat in the seasoned flour.

3 Heat the oil to 375°F. Dip the fish pieces in the batter and then fry in the hot oil for 3-4 minutes. Drain and dry on absorbent paper. Serve with mayonnaise dips, vegetable salads, and a tartar, horseradish or chili sauce.

Serves 4

Tartar Sauce
Blend ⅔ cup mayonnaise with 1 tablespoon chopped parsley, dill pickles and capers.

Horseradish Sauce
Blend ⅔ cup mayonnaise with 1 tablespoon grated horseradish.

Chili Sauce
Blend ⅔ cup mayonnaise with ½ teaspoon Tabasco sauce and 1 tablespoon chopped chives.

Red Pepper Dip

2 tablespoons soy sauce
1 teaspoon vinegar
juice 1 orange
1 small onion, finely chopped
salt and pepper
1 teaspoon sugar
⅔ cup mayonnaise
scant ½ cup finely chopped sweet red pepper
3 tangerine sections

1 Mix together the soy sauce, vinegar, orange juice, onion, salt and pepper and sugar in a blender or a bowl.

2 Lightly blend in the mayonnaise, then add the red pepper and tangerine sections.

Makes ⅔ cup

Pineapple Dip

⅔ cup mayonnaise or salad dressing
2 tablespoons chopped pineapple
2 tablespoons soy sauce
1 clove garlic, chopped
⅓ cup pineapple juice

1 Work all the ingredients, except the mayonnaise or salad dressing, in a blender or in a bowl.

2 Blend in the mayonnaise or salad dressing.

Makes ⅔ cup

Fish-balls Chinese-style

1 onion, peeled
1 lb. white fish (e.g. haddock, cod, sole) skinned and bones removed

2 cups crushed saltines or breadcrumbs
1 teaspoon sugar
salt and pepper
1 egg, beaten
½ cup seasoned flour
oil for deep frying

For the Batter:
1 egg
1 cup + 2 tablespoons flour
⅔ cup flat beer or water

1 Combine the ingredients for the batter in a bowl to form a smooth but fairly liquid batter. Leave for 20 minutes before using.

2 Grate the onion into a bowl. Grind the fish and add to the onion. Blend in the crushed crackers or breadcrumbs, sugar, salt and pepper to taste and the beaten egg. Grind again to obtain a smooth paste.

3 Divide the mixture into small dumplings and coat with seasoned flour, then dip in the batter.

4 Heat the oil to 375°F. Then fry the dumplings a few at a time for 3 minutes or until crisp and golden. Drain on absorbent paper. Serve at once with a sweet 'n sour sauce.

Serves 4

Vegetable accompaniments
You can serve almost any raw vegetables with Fish Tempura, such as carrots, turnips and cucumber, all cut in floral shapes. All vegetables must be raw or, at the most, scalded, so that they keep their color and taste. To scald, plunge into boiling salted water for 30 seconds.

Fish Tempura — small pieces of fish cooked quickly in hot oil and served with various vegetables and sauces

Beer Batter

2¼ cups flour
pinch salt
⅔ cup flat beer
1 egg yolk
⅔ cup milk
2 egg whites
2 tablespoons oil

1 Sift the flour and salt into a bowl.

2 Mix the beer, egg yolk and milk together and then blend this mixture into the flour to obtain a smooth batter. Cover the bowl with a cloth and let the batter stand at room temperature for 1 hour.

3 When the batter is ready, beat the egg whites until they stand in soft peaks. Add the egg whites and the oil to the batter and use immediately.

Makes about 1¼ cups

Fish Fritters. The recipe for Beer Batter given above can be used to coat all kinds of fish, meat and vegetables for deep-frying.

French Fried Onions

1 lb. large onions, sliced across in rings
⅔ cup milk
½ cup flour
salt
oil for deep frying

1 Separate the onion slices into rings. Place the rings in a bowl, cover with cold water and soak for 10 minutes. Drain well.

2 Dip the onion rings in the milk and then drain in a colander. Sift the flour and a pinch of salt onto a plate. Coat the onion rings in the seasoned flour.

3 Heat the oil to 375°F. Add the onion rings and fry for 3 minutes or until golden. Drain them on absorbent paper and use as a garnish for deep-fried fish.

Makes about 1 lb.

French Fried Parsley

bunch parsley
oil for deep frying

1 Wash the parsley well, drain and dry on a cloth. The parsley must be as free from moisture as possible.

2 Heat the oil to 400°F. and add the parsley sprigs. Allow them to fry for only 15 to 20 seconds. Drain and dry on absorbent paper. Use for garnishing fried fish.

Rolled Scrod

4 scrod (young cod)
2 eggs
2 tablespoons oil
salt and pepper
1 cup flour
3 slices fresh bread
oil for deep frying
few sprigs parsley

1 Trim, clean and wash the scrod. Carefully split them along the backbone with a filleting knife. Slip the filleting knife through to separate the two fillets. Cut out the backbone close to the head with kitchen scissors. Dry the fillets.

2 Prepare the coating. Put the eggs, oil and some salt and pepper in a deep plate. Beat with a whisk. Spread the flour on a plate. Make crumbs from the bread, and pour onto another plate.

3 Dip the scrod successively in the flour, the beaten egg and the breadcrumbs. Press on the crumbs gently with the blade of a knife, then roll up the fillets to the outside of either side of the head. Keep them in place with a skewer or wooden toothpick. (See step-by-step, pages 426-427.)

4 Heat the oil in the deep fat fryer to 375°F.

5 Carefully lower the rolled-up scrod into the hot oil and fry until golden-brown. Drain them on absorbent paper and keep hot.

6 Toss the parsley into the oil and fry for 2 seconds. Drain and decorate the serving dish with it. Serve with a tomato sauce.

Serves 4

Fried Smelts

1 lb. smelts
1 cup + 2 tablespoons flour
1 cup milk or beer
oil for deep frying
1 bunch parsley
2 lemons
salt

1 Clean, wash and dry the fish.

2 Pour the flour into a bowl.

3 Put the fish in a deep dish and soak in the milk or beer.

4 Heat the oil in a deep fat fryer to 375°F.

5 Drain the fish in a colander. Shake them, then toss them in the flour. It is best to do this gradually so the flour does not get too wet and clot on the fish. Toss the fish so that they are evenly covered. Then empty them back into the dried colander to remove any excess flour. Wash and dry the parsley. Cut the lemons into quarters.

6 Put the fish into the frying basket and lower into the hot oil. When the fish are golden and have risen to the surface, drain and dry them on absorbent paper. Add salt.

7 Fry the parsley for 2 or 3 seconds. Drain it.

8 Heat a serving dish. Put the fish on it. Decorate with the fried parsley and lemon quarters. Serve immediately.

Serves 4

Tip: It is not practical to clean very small fish, but they should be thoroughly washed.

1 Put the smelts in a container and cover with milk. For a variety of flavor, some of the fish can be soaked in beer in a separate container **2** Pour the flour into another container. Drain the fish and then, with the hands, toss them in the flour **3** Put the fish in a perforated basket (the one from the fryer, for example). Shake the fish to remove any excess flour **4** The fish are now ready for frying **5** Heat the oil. Lower the

basket into the hot, but not smoking oil **6** When the fish are cooked, raise the basket and rest the loops on the handles of the fryer, so that the oil can drain **7** Dry the fish on absorbent paper, put them onto a plate and lightly salt them **8** Fry the parsley in the same oil **9** Arrange the fish on a hot serving dish. Decorate with the parsley and lemons cut into quarters

Look 'n Cook Fried Fish Fingers

1 Take fillets of cod or haddock. Cut them into long pieces (fingers). Marinate them in the oil, lemon and parsley mixture 2 Prepare the batter 3 Beat the egg whites until stiff and fold into the batter 4 Heat up the frying oil. Drain the pieces of fish. Dip them in the batter 5 Lower them into the hot oil and let them brown 6 Drain and serve with fried parsley

Fish Croquettes

1 tablespoon oil
1 onion, chopped
1 shallot, chopped
1 cup mushrooms, chopped
2 sprigs parsley, chopped
1 cup milk
¼ cup flour
salt and pepper
freshly grated nutmeg
1 cup ground fish fillets (any white fish)
oil for deep frying

1 Heat the oil in a pan, add the chopped vegetables and parsley and cook gently without browning. Warm the milk.

2 Stir in half the flour and cook for a few seconds, stirring constantly with a wooden spoon.

3 Stir in the milk gradually. Season with salt and pepper to taste and add a little grated nutmeg.

4 Stir in the ground fish and cook gently for 10 minutes, stirring constantly. Remove from the heat and leave to cool.

5 Heat the oil to 375°F.

6 Shape the fish mixture into croquettes, then roll them in the remaining flour.

7 Deep-fry the croquettes in the hot oil until golden, then drain on absorbent paper and serve hot with a tomato sauce.

Serves 4

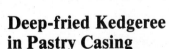

Deep-fried Kedgeree in Pastry Casing

¼ lb. flaked cooked haddock
⅓ cup cooked rice
½ cup cooked peas
⅔ cup diced cooked carrots
⅓ cup canned baked beans in tomato sauce
⅓ cup chopped raw onion
1 hard-boiled egg, coarsely chopped

salt and pepper
pinch curry powder
½ lb. puff pastry, homemade or frozen and thawed
oil for deep frying

1 Place the haddock, rice, peas, carrots, baked beans, onion, egg, salt, pepper and curry powder in a bowl and mix thoroughly.

2 Roll out the puff pastry thinly (⅛ inch thick). Cut the pastry into 4 rounds, each about 6 inches in diameter.

3 Place 3 large spoonfuls of the kedgeree mixture on each pastry round. Brush the edges of the pastry with water and fold over to make a half-moon shape and enclose the stuffing. Press the edges together to seal.

4 Heat the oil to 375°F. Add the pastry cases and fry for 4 minutes or until golden.

5 Drain and serve with tomato curry sauce or lemon wedges.

Serves 4

Indian Fish Cutlets

3 cups cooked rice
½ lb. any cooked fish
2 tablespoons curry powder
3 eggs
salt and pepper
1 cup fresh breadcrumbs
5 tablespoons shredded coconut
1 cup + 2 tablespoons seasoned flour
oil for deep frying

1 Grind the rice and fish together twice. Add the curry powder, 1 egg and seasoning and mix well. Form the mixture into 4 cutlet shapes.

2 Beat the remaining eggs. Mix the breadcrumbs and shredded coconut. Coat the cutlets in the seasoned flour, then dip in the beaten egg and then roll in the breadcrumbs.

3 Heat the oil to 375°F, add the cutlets and fry for 5 minutes. Serve with a wedge of lemon.

Serves 4

Fried Cod Fingers

1 lemon
2 lbs. cod fillets, skinned
¼ cup oil
¼ cup chopped parsley and chervil
freshly ground pepper and salt
oil for frying

For the Batter:
1 cup + 2 tablespoons flour
2 eggs, separated
½ cup beer

1 Squeeze the lemon. Cut the cod fillets into strips (fingers). Place in an earthenware dish. Pour the lemon juice and the oil over them. Sprinkle with the chopped parsley and chervil, some pepper and a little salt. Mix very carefully and leave to soak.

2 Pour the flour into a bowl. Put the egg yolks into the middle with a pinch of salt. Using a whisk, mix in the flour a little at a time. When the batter becomes too thick, dilute it with the beer to obtain a type of thick pancake batter. Let stand.

3 Meanwhile, beat the egg whites until firm. Add to the batter and fold in with a metal spoon or spatula, giving a very light batter. Heat the oil in a deep fat fryer to 375°F.

4 Drain the cod strips well, dip into the batter and lower into the hot oil.

5 Drain the strips on absorbent paper when they are golden. Serve immediately, very hot, with mayonnaise, a tartar sauce or fried parsley.

Serves 6

443

Baked Fish

Baking Fish

Baking is one of the most versatile methods of cooking. Fish may be baked simply, with a little butter, lemon juice and parsley; in a variety of different liquids such as stock, wine, apple cider, or cream; or stuffed, in a rich sauce. Baking retains the flavor of the fish supremely well, and cooking smells are kept to a minimum.

Arrange the fish attractively in a casserole — which can also be used as a serving dish. Always preheat the oven. Set it at 350°F. for dishes to be cooked in a covered casserole; 400°F. if you want a golden brown or gratinéed surface.

The possibilities for experimenting with different ingredients, herbs and seasonings are almost limitless. Sousing is a form of baking: cook at 350°F. and allow the fish to cool in spiced vinegar.

Cooked 'en papillote,' the fish is placed on a sheet of aluminum foil or parchment paper, covered with a garnish, rich or simple. The sheet is folded to make an airtight parcel and the fish cooks in its own juices in the oven. Serve the fish in its wrapping on each plate. This method of cooking is excellent as part of a calorie-controlled diet.

A popular American method of cooking fish is 'planking.' The fish is partially grilled or broiled, then transferred to an oiled oak plank, and baked. The plank imparts a delicious, barbecue-like flavor and aroma — and makes an impressive dish to present to guests, especially if the platter is decorated with a piped border of duchesse potatoes before it is placed in the oven.

Serve boiled or creamed potatoes with baked fish — or make a rice pilaf. A crisp green salad is an excellent accompaniment.

Baked Fish Fillets in Sour Cream

four 5-oz. fish fillets
salt and pepper
¼ cup oil
¼ cup chopped chives
⅔ cup sour cream
1 bay leaf
pinch caraway seeds (optional)
pinch paprika
sprig parsley
4 lemon wedges

1 Set the oven at 400°F.

2 Place the fish fillets on a buttered, shallow dish. Season with salt and pepper and brush with oil. Bake for 5 minutes in the preheated oven.

3 Add the chopped chives, sour cream, bay leaf and caraway seeds, cover with a lid, return to the oven and bake for 15 minutes at the same temperature.

4 Serve the fish in the same dish, with boiled new potatoes and turnips. Sprinkle with paprika just before serving and decorate with parsley and lemon wedges.

Serves 4

Baked Mackerel Stuffed with Apple

four ½-lb. mackerel
¼ lb. butter
1 cup celery, finely chopped
1 apple, peeled and finely chopped
small onion, chopped

1 cup fresh breadcrumbs
1 tablespoon chopped parsley
salt and pepper
pinch ground ginger
juice and grated rind 1 lemon

1 Preheat the oven to 350°F.

2 Using a sharp knife, remove the backbones from the fish without damaging the flesh. Open out the fish to form a pocket for the stuffing, and clean it thoroughly.

3 Make the stuffing. Melt ¼ cup butter in a saucepan and sauté the celery, apple and onion for 4 minutes. Stir in the breadcrumbs and chopped parsley. Season with salt and pepper and add the ginger, grated lemon rind and juice.

4 Spread the filling evenly on each mackerel, and fold over. Melt the remaining butter in a pan and use to brush the mackerel. Wrap them in foil and bake in the oven for 20 minutes.

Serves 4

Baking en Papillote

A papillote is a heart-shaped piece of parchment paper or aluminum foil, well-oiled or buttered, and folded around the ingredients to be cooked. This method of cooking is advantageous because it ensures that the fish simmers in its own juices and thus does not lose its own distinctive flavor.

Many fish can be cooked in this way — trout, red mullet, sole or pompano to name but a few. Really, the term only implies half-cooking because the fish used is often precooked before it is placed in the paper bag or foil.

Always serve papillotes in their puffed-up paper shells and let your guests cut them open themselves at the table with a knife. If you use aluminum foil, remove the fish from the foil to serve.

Red Mullet en Papillote

four ½-lb. red mullet
¼ cup butter
1 cup mushrooms,
 chopped
1 cup onions, chopped
8 thin slices ham
¼ cup oil

1 Preheat the oven to 350°F.

2 Clean and wash the fish.

3 Heat the butter in a skillet and sauté the mushrooms and onions for 5 minutes.

4 Take 4 sheets of parchment paper and fold each sheet in half 14 inches wide. Cut each sheet into a heart shape.

5 Place a slice of ham in the center of each heart and add a spoonful of the cooked mushrooms and onions. Arrange the fish on top and coat with a little more mushroom mixture. Cover with another slice of ham.

6 Fold over the left side of the paper and roll the two edges up together to make a sealed paper bag. Start from inside the top of the heart and, with small, even movements, twist until the envelope is firmly closed. Brush the outside of each envelope with oil.

7 Place the paper bags on a well-oiled tray and bake in the oven for 20 minutes. Serve with a tomato sauce.

Serves 4

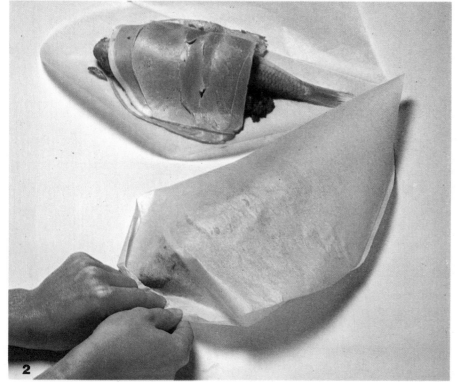

1 Place a slice of ham on a cut-out, heart-shaped, oiled piece of parchment paper. Place the fish on top and spoon over sautéed mushrooms and onions. **2** Cover with another slice of ham and fold over the paper. Seal up the edges between your finger and thumb and place in the oven for 20 minutes. **3** Serve the red mullet in its paper bag

Polynesian Baked Mackerel

four ½-lb. mackerel
salt and pepper
¼ cup butter
2 cups mushrooms, sliced
1 sprig thyme
1 bay leaf
1 lemon

For the Marinade:
⅔ cup pineapple juice
⅔ cup dry white wine
1 tablespoon soy sauce
1 clove garlic, crushed
1 medium onion, chopped
salt and pepper
1 teaspoon sugar

1 Preheat the oven to 400°F.

2 Clean and wash the fish. Make 4 slits in each mackerel. Season with salt and pepper and place in a shallow dish.

3 Place all the ingredients for the marinade in a blender and blend. Transfer the marinade to a pan and boil for 5 minutes.

4 Slice the mushrooms and heat the butter in a small pan. Add the mushrooms and sauté for 1 minute and place around the fish, with thyme and bay leaf.

5 Pour on the marinade and bake in the oven for 25 minutes. Baste with the liquid from time to time.

6 Serve with wedges of lemon.

Serves 4

---

*Polynesian Baked Mackerel —
the mackerel are marinated in
pineapple juice and white wine
and baked with mushrooms*

Portuguese Stuffed Flounder Rolls

eight ¼-lb. fillets of flounder or
   lemon sole, skinned
¼ cup butter
½ lb. cooked, peeled, deveined
   jumbo shrimp
1 lemon

For the Stuffing:
1 hard-boiled egg
1 sprig watercress
¼ cup butter
¼ cup oil
1 onion, chopped
2 cups fresh breadcrumbs
1 egg, beaten
juice and grated rind 1 lemon
salt and pepper

For the Sauce:
1¼ cups velouté sauce
1 tablespoon tomato paste
2 tablespoons dry sherry
juice ½ lemon
salt and pepper

1 Preheat the oven to 350°F.

2 Tap each fillet gently with a rolling pin to break down the fibers.

3 Chop the hard-boiled egg and watercress and mix well with the other stuffing ingredients to form a paste.

4 Spread the stuffing evenly over each fish fillet. Roll up the fillets and place upright in a shallow oven-proof dish. Season, dot with butter and bake for 15 minutes.

5 Meanwhile, make the sauce. Boil the velouté and stir in the tomato paste, sherry and lemon juice. Season to taste.

6 Pour the sauce over the cooked, rolled fillets and decorate with the shrimp and lemon wedges.

Serves 4

---

*Portuguese Stuffed Flounder
Rolls are stuffed with breadcrumbs, watercress and lemon
and then covered in a
sherry sauce*

Mexican Baked Cod

four ½-lb. cod steaks
salt and pepper
⅔ cup medium dry sherry
¼ cup grapefruit juice
pinch paprika
bouquet garni
¼ cup oil and butter
1 onion, chopped
4 tomatoes, skinned, seeded and
  chopped
1 red pepper, seeded and
  chopped
¾ cup corn kernels
1 cup fresh breadcrumbs
1 tablespoon chopped parsley

1 Preheat the oven to 400 F.

2 Wash and dry the cod steaks. Season with salt and pepper and place in a shallow ovenproof dish. Pour on the sherry and grapefruit juice. Add a pinch of paprika and the bouquet garni.

3 Bake in the oven for 15 minutes.

4 Meanwhile, heat the butter and oil in a saucepan and sauté the chopped onions until soft. Add the tomatoes, red pepper and corn. Season with salt and pepper and simmer for 8 minutes.

5 When the fish are cooked, remove from the oven. Place the cod steaks on a serving dish and keep warm. Drain off the fish liquor and add to the sauce.

6 Boil the sauce for 4 minutes,

Mexican Baked Cod — the cod steaks are cooked in sherry and grapefruit juice and served in a tomato sauce

season to taste and remove from the heat. Stir in the breadcrumbs and chopped parsley, and pour over the cod steaks.

7 Serve with boiled potatoes or rice.

Serves 4

Herring with Apples in Cider

2 lbs. fresh herring, filleted
½ cup flour
1 tablespoon prepared mustard
salt and pepper
1 onion, sliced
2 apples, peeled and sliced in
  rings
3 cups potatoes, thinly sliced
1¼ cups apple cider
1¼ cups water
1 tablespoon cider vinegar
1 bay leaf
¼ lb. butter
1 tablespoon chopped parsley

1 Preheat the oven to 400°F.

2 Wash and drain the herring fillets and coat with flour. Spread the mustard on the fleshy side. Season with salt and pepper.

3 Place the fish fillets, side by side, in an oblong, shallow dish and cover with alternate layers of sliced onion, apples and potatoes. Season with salt and pepper.

4 Pour in the apple cider, water and cider vinegar. Add the bay leaf and dot the top with small pieces of butter.

5 Bake in the oven for 45-50 minutes. Sprinkle with parsley before serving.

Serves 4

Baked & Braised Fish

Halibut in Wine

four $\frac{1}{2}$-lb. halibut steaks, about 1
  inch thick
$\frac{1}{2}$ lemon
salt and pepper
1 tablespoon oil
$\frac{2}{3}$ cup dry vermouth

$1\frac{1}{2}$ cups heavy cream
$\frac{1}{4}$ cup butter
$\frac{1}{2}$ lb. button mushrooms, sliced
1 onion, chopped
$\frac{1}{4}$ lb. cooked, peeled, deveined
  shrimp
2 tablespoons tomato paste
pinch cayenne pepper
1 tablespoon brandy

1 Preheat the oven to 400°F. Rub the steaks with the lemon. Salt and pepper lightly.

2 Place the fish steaks in an oiled ovenproof dish and pour over the vermouth and $1\frac{1}{4}$ cups heavy cream.

3 Cover the dish with aluminum foil and place in the preheated oven for 20 minutes.

4 Heat 2 tablespoons butter in a pan, add the mushrooms and sauté for 2 minutes. Add salt and pepper and the rest of the cream. Keep warm.

5 In a separate pan, melt the rest of the butter, add the onion and mushrooms and sauté, covered, for 6 minutes. Add the remaining ingredients and cook for 2 minutes. Add the cream. Taste and correct the seasoning.

6 Transfer the halibut to a warm serving dish and cover with the sauce. Serve with boiled potatoes and a green salad.

Serves 6

Halibut in Wine — halibut baked with shrimp in a rich, creamy sauce flavored with vermouth and brandy

Baked Bass with Mushroom and Olive Stuffing

one 4-lb. bass, cleaned, scaled
1¼ cups dry white wine
1¼ cups water
1 onion, sliced
1 carrot, sliced
bouquet garni
1 clove garlic, crushed
1 bulb fennel, sliced
salt and pepper

For the Stuffing:
¼ cup oil
1 onion, chopped
½ lb. chopped mushrooms
4 cups fresh breadcrumbs
1 tablespoon chopped parsley
4 pitted olives, chopped

For the Garnish:
6 mushrooms

6 black olives, pitted
6 green olives, pitted
4 tomatoes
1 lemon

1 Preheat the oven to 400°F. Place the bass in a shallow ovenproof dish and add the wine, water, onion, carrot, bouquet garni, garlic, fennel and seasoning. Cover with parchment paper and bake in the preheated oven for 30 minutes.

2 Remove the dish from the oven, discard the bouquet garni and lift out the vegetables. Chop them coarsely and put on one side to use in the stuffing. Place the fish on an oval serving dish and reserve the stock. Reduce the oven temperature to 350°F.

3 Make the stuffing: heat the oil in a pan and add the chopped onion and mushrooms. Cook for 5 minutes and then add the chopped, cooked vegetables, the bread-crumbs, salt and pepper, parsley and chopped olives. Mix well.

4 Cut the tops of the mushrooms in swirls using a zesting knife and then boil the mushrooms for 4 minutes in a little of the reserved fish stock.

5 Surround the bass with the stuffing. Decorate with the black and green olives and the cooked mushrooms.

6 Place the 4 tomatoes for the garnish in boiling water for 1 minute, remove and peel off the skins. Cut the lemon in a decorative shape and

---

Baked Bass with Mushroom and Olive Stuffing is served surrounded by stuffing, and garnished with peeled tomatoes, olives and lemon waterlilies

place the tomatoes and lemon on the dish. Return the dish to the oven for 12 minutes to heat. Serve with boiled potatoes.

Serves 6

Bass or Snapper à la Dugleré

one 2-lb. bass or snapper, cleaned
   and scaled
¼ cup butter
4 tomatoes, skinned, seeded and
   chopped
2 onions, chopped
2 shallots, chopped
1 clove garlic, chopped
bouquet garni

salt and pepper
1¼ cups dry white wine
2 tablespoons flour
pinch cayenne pepper
1 tablespoon chopped parsley

1 Wash and dry the fish. Either leave it whole or cut it into 6 steaks. Do not separate these but leave them together.

2 Preheat the oven to 375°F. Liberally butter an oval ovenproof dish with 1 tablespoon of the butter. Arrange half the chopped tomatoes, onions and shallots and the bouquet garni on the bottom of the dish. Place the fish on top. Cover it with the rest of the tomatoes, onions and shallots. Season with salt and pepper. Sprinkle the wine over the top. Cut 2 tablespoons of the butter into small pieces and scatter them over the fish. Cook in the preheated oven for 30 minutes.

3 When the fish is cooked, transfer it carefully from the cooking dish to

The ingredients for Bass or Snapper Dugleré. The bass is cooked in white wine, with tomatoes and shallots

---

a heated oval serving dish. Keep warm.

4 Pour the cooking juices and vegetables into a saucepan and bring to a boil. Boil until reduced by one-quarter. Discard the bouquet garni. Knead the rest of the butter with the flour to make a paste. Whisk this into the cooking juices and simmer until thickened.

5 Correct the seasoning and add the cayenne pepper.

6 Coat the fish with the sauce and serve immediately, sprinkled with the chopped parsley.

Serves 4

Look 'n Cook Stuffed Fish Boat-style

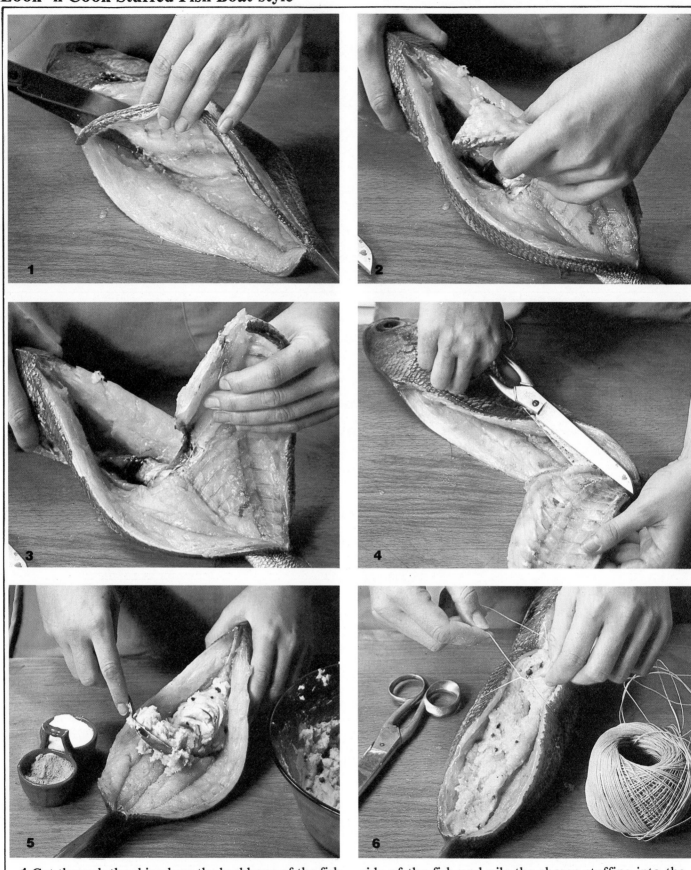

1 Cut through the skin along the backbone of the fish and loosen the fillets on either side of the central section **2, 3** and **4** Detach the central section, pulling it from the head toward the tail, cutting through at the base of the tail using a pair of scissors **5** Season the in-side of the fish and pile the chosen stuffing into the cavity **6** Close the two sides of the fish and tie with kitchen string, making sure that the string is not too tight. The fish is now ready for cooking

Cider Baked Red Mullet

12 red mullet fillets
salt and pepper
1¼ cups apple cider
1 tablespoon mixed pickling spice
4 bay leaves
2 small onions, cut in rings

1 Preheat the oven to 350°F. Wash and dry the fish and season well with salt and pepper. Roll up the fillets, skin inward, beginning at the tail end. Place fairly close together in an ovenproof dish.

2 Cover the fish with the apple cider and sprinkle with the pickling spice. Place the bay leaves and the onion rings on top.

3 Cover the dish with aluminum foil and cook in the preheated oven for about 1 hour.

Serves 4-6

Farmer's Casserole

four ½-lb. fillets red snapper, perch or bass
6 tablespoons butter
2 large onions, sliced
4 medium potatoes, thinly sliced
salt and pepper

1 Preheat the oven to 400°F. Wash and dry the fillets. Use 2 tablespoons of the butter to grease an ovenproof dish and then place the fillets in the bottom.

2 Cover the fish with a layer of onion slices and then a layer of potato slices. Season and dot with butter. Cover with another layer of onions and potatoes, season again and dot the rest of the butter over the top.

3 Cover the dish with a lid or aluminum foil and bake in the preheated oven for 20 minutes.

4 Remove the lid or foil, and replace in the oven for 5 minutes to brown the potatoes.

Serves 4

Tip: Instead of potatoes, try using the same amount of sliced Jerusalem artichokes, turnips and cooked shell pasta. Sprinkle with grated cheese and bake uncovered.

Stuffed Trout Cooked in Foil

four ½-lb. trout, cleaned
1½ tablespoons butter
3 shallots or 1 onion, finely chopped
½ lb. chopped mushrooms
⅔ cup light cream
salt and pepper
⅓ cup dried white breadcrumbs
1 tablespoon chopped fresh chervil
1 tablespoon chopped fresh parsley
1 egg

1 Preheat the oven to 400°F. Rinse and dry the fish.

2 Prepare the stuffing: melt the butter in a heavy-based skillet. Add the shallots or onion and cook until softened. Add the mushrooms and cook until the mixture is quite dry.

3 Stir in the cream and add salt and pepper to taste. Simmer gently until reduced by half, stirring occasionally.

4 Remove from the heat and add the breadcrumbs, chervil, parsley and egg. Mix well and season to taste with salt and pepper.

5 Divide this stuffing between the trout and spread it inside them. Leave until cold. Close the openings and secure with string (see step-by-step illustrations opposite). Wrap each trout in foil. Arrange on a rack in a roasting pan and cook in the preheated oven for 20 minutes.

6 Serve the trout in the foil.

Serves 4

Tip: Pats of butter, either plain or flavored, can be placed on top of the fish when unwrapped.

Baked Red Snapper Provençale

1 tablespoon butter
2 small onions, cut in wedges
3 tomatoes, skinned and cut in wedges
1 teaspoon sugar
salt and pepper
2 tablespoons vinegar
four ½-lb. red snapper (or bluefish)
1 tablespoon chopped parsley

1 Heat 2 tablespoons of the butter in a skillet, add the onions and sauté for about 5 minutes. Preheat the oven to 375°F.

2 Using half of the remaining butter, grease an ovenproof dish. Place the tomatoes and fried onions in the bottom and then sprinkle with the sugar. Add salt, plenty of pepper and the vinegar. Arrange the fish fillets on top.

3 In a small saucepan, warm the rest of the butter and brush the fish with the melted butter.

4 Cover the dish with a lid or aluminum foil and bake in the preheated oven for 20 minutes. Serve sprinkled with the chopped parsley.

Serves 4

Tip: To pep up the flavor, add ½ lb. strips of red and green pepper and a pinch of garlic salt and curry powder.

Baked Cod Icelandic Style

one 3-lb. cod, gutted
2 lemons
salt and pepper
¼ cup butter, softened
1 large onion, sliced
2 large carrots, sliced
bouquet garni
1 clove garlic, crushed
2 tablespoons vinegar
2 cups water
1 chicken bouillon cube
½ cup light cream
1 teaspoon cornstarch
2 sprigs parsley

1 Preheat the oven to 400°F.

2 Clean and wash the fish and remove the head and fins if necessary. Make several slits at regular intervals along the backbone with a sharp knife.

3 Cut one lemon in half lengthwise and then slice thinly. Insert a lemon slice in each slit and season.

4 Rub the fish with the softened butter and place in a large pan. Add the sliced onion rings, carrots, bouquet garni and garlic. Pour in the vinegar and water and sprinkle with the crumbled bouillon cube. Bake in the oven for 45 minutes.

5 When the fish is cooked, strain off the fish liquor into a saucepan and boil it to reduce by half. Keep the fish warm.

6 Mix together the cream and cornstarch and add to the fish stock to thicken it. Heat without boiling.

7 Garnish the cod with lemon wedges and parsley sprigs. Serve on a large serving plate surrounded by boiled and roast potatoes, sprouts, baby carrots and green beans. Serve the sauce separately.

Serves 6

Baked Cod Icelandic Style — the cod is baked whole, served with boiled potatoes, carrots, sprouts and green beans

Fish with Pastry

Salmon and Shrimp Pastry Slice

1 lb. puff pastry, frozen and
  thawed
$\frac{1}{4}$ lb. thinly sliced smoked salmon
  (lox)
$\frac{1}{4}$ lb. cooked, peeled, deveined
  shrimp
1 tablespoon chopped parsley
1 lemon, cut lengthwise and sliced
1 sprig dill

For the Mushroom Sauce Filling:
$\frac{2}{3}$ cup thick white sauce
1 cup mushrooms
  chopped and lightly salted
1 teaspoon anchovy paste
pinch paprika
salt and pepper
juice $\frac{1}{2}$ lemon
$\frac{1}{2}$ cup grated Cheddar or Parmesan
  cheese

For the Salmon Filling:
$\frac{1}{4}$ lb. cooked, peeled shrimp
$\frac{2}{3}$ cup mayonnaise
$\frac{1}{4}$ lb. smoked salmon trimmings,
  chopped

1 Preheat the oven to 400°F.

2 Roll out the puff pastry to $\frac{1}{8}$ inch
thick. Cut out three circles, 8 inches
in diameter.

3 Place the pastry circles on a buttered baking sheet and prick the
pastry several times with a fork.
Bake in the oven for 15 minutes.

4 Meanwhile, prepare the fillings.
Heat the white sauce in a pan and
stir in the chopped mushrooms, anchovy paste and paprika. Simmer

for 5 minutes, then season to taste.
Add the lemon juice and cool a little before stirring in the grated
cheese.

5 Blend the shrimp with $\frac{1}{2}$ cup
mayonnaise. Stir in the smoked
salmon trimmings, making sure
that all bones and skin have been
removed.

6 When the pastry slices are cool,
place one layer on a large, round
plate and spread thickly with the
mushroom sauce. Top with another
slice and cover with most of the
smoked salmon mixture — reserve
a little for the cornets. Place the
third slice on top and coat with the
remaining mayonnaise.

7 Roll up the smoked salmon slices
into cornet shapes and fill with the
remaining smoked salmon mixture.
Arrange the cornets on top of the
pastry slice.

8 Decorate with peeled shrimp and
sprinkle with the chopped parsley
and dill. Arrange the lemon slices
and sprig of dill in the center. Chill
in the refrigerator for 30 minutes
before serving.

Serves 6

*Salmon and Shrimp Pastry
Slice—alternate layers of smoked
salmon and shrimp and
mushroom sauce*

Salmon Loaf

6⅓ cups water
pinch salt
½ cup long grain rice
½ lb. salmon, drained
1 sweet red pepper, seeded and
  chopped
10 pitted green olives
4 hard-boiled eggs, chopped
¼ cup mayonnaise
1 teaspoon tomato paste
juice ½ lemon
¼ cup butter, softened
1 small head lettuce, washed and
  diced
small pinch parsley

1 Boil the water in a saucepan and add the salt and rice. Cook for about 20-25 minutes, drain and cool.

2 Flake the salmon with a fork. Add the chopped red pepper and olives, rice and hard-boiled eggs.

3 Blend the mayonnaise with the tomato paste and lemon juice, and stir in the salmon mixture.

4 Butter inside an oblong mold (or cake pan) with the butter. Pour in the salmon mixture, pressing it down well. Chill in the refrigerator for 2 hours.

5 Cover a serving platter with the lettuce leaves and turn out the salmon loaf onto them. Decorate with parsley and serve immediately.

Serves 4

Salmon Pastry Envelopes

½ lb. mushrooms, chopped
juice ½ lemon
1 lb. canned salmon
¼ cup butter

6 shallots or onions, peeled and
  chopped
¼ cup flour
½ cup light cream
2 eggs, beaten
4 sprigs parsley, chopped
1 lb. puff pastry, frozen and
  thawed

1 Preheat the oven to 350°F.

2 Place the chopped mushrooms in a small bowl and marinate in the lemon juice.

3 Drain the salmon and put aside the fish juice in a small bowl. Remove the bones and pound the flesh finely with a rolling pin or pestle.

4 Heat the butter in a skillet. Add the shallots or onions and the mushrooms which have been soaked in lemon juice. Sauté for 3 minutes, then add the salmon, stirring briskly over high heat.

5 Stir in the flour and cook for 3 minutes, then add the salmon juice and cream, stirring all the time. Stir in 1 beaten egg and the chopped parsley when the sauce has thickened, and remove from the heat.

6 Roll out the puff pastry ⅛ inch thick and cut into rectangles 3 inches across by 4 inches long.

7 Place some of the salmon filling on the middle of each rectangle and moisten the pastry edges. Fold over and pinch together to seal the parcels. Brush with beaten egg.

8 Place the parcels on a greased baking sheet and bake for 15-20 minutes. Serve hot or cold.

Serves 6

Coulibiac

Coulibiac is a traditional, hot, Russian fish pie usually made with salmon. It is served with sour cream.

¼ cup butter
1 medium onion, chopped
1 cup long grain rice
4¼ cups water
1 chicken bouillon cube
2 lbs. puff pastry, frozen and
  thawed
½ lb. salmon, flaked
juice 1 lemon
1¼ cups mushrooms, sliced
salt and pepper
2 hard-boiled eggs, sliced
1 egg, beaten

1 Preheat the oven to 400°F.

2 Heat the butter in a saucepan and sauté the onion until soft. Add the rice and simmer for 3 minutes until transparent. Add the water and crumble in the bouillon cube. Bring to a boil, then simmer for 20 minutes, until the rice is cooked.

3 Roll out the pastry into an oblong shape on a floured board until it is ⅛ thick. Place a layer of the cooked rice in the center, then a layer of salmon. Pour on the lemon juice and top with the sliced mushrooms. Season with salt and pepper. Cover with more rice and arrange the slices of hard-boiled eggs along the top.

4 Wrap the pastry over so that it resembles a bread loaf and place on a greased baking sheet. Brush the top with beaten egg and make a decorative pattern with a fork.

5 Bake in the oven for 30 minutes. Serve with a dish of sour cream or shrimp sauce.

Serves 6

Tips: Coulibiac can be served with a sour cream sauce — *smitana*. To make this, just boil up a few shallots in a cup of white wine, stir in some sour cream and season with salt and pepper.

Another way to make Coulibiac is to use biscuit dough instead of puff pastry.

Coulibiac is a traditional Russian pie stuffed with salmon, rice and eggs

Freshwater Fish

Freshwater fish are found in lakes and rivers. They include the sedentary fish such as carp, bass, pike, and also the migratory trout, salmon, and eels. America is rich in freshwater fish. Use catfish, yellow perch, pickerel and substitute local fish for those suggested in the recipes, where appropriate.

The sedentary river fish tend to have a muddy flavor and must be soaked in cold water before cooking. Fish from flowing freshwater or spring water can be very tasty, especially if smoked. Some freshwater fish such as salmon and sturgeon have excellent roes which, when salted, can be made into caviar.

Always serve savory, rich sauces with sedentary fish. Or mince them and make into dumplings or 'quenelles.' The sauces served with 'quenelles' are usually flavored with shellfish. Crayfish, a kind of large river shrimp with claws, is often used in the South.

Most cooking methods used for marine fish are also suitable for freshwater fish. Large, round fish such as salmon can be cut into steaks across the bone. The smaller flat fish can be filleted. Salmon and trout are best poached in a 'court bouillon' (a fish stock) and can then be served either hot or cold. A whole, cold salmon in aspic makes a magnificent centerpiece for a buffet or party.

Freshwater Fish

- Bass
- Carp
- Catfish
- Eel
- Perch
- Pickerel
- Pike
- Salmon
- Trout

Poached Trout — the trout is poached in a court bouillon and served whole with lemon wedges and Hollandaise sauce

Serving poached fish

Serve poached freshwater fish in their own court bouillon in a shallow dish. The court bouillon should always be clear — never cloudy. Serve with sliced carrots, sliced cooked onions and boiled potatoes and garnish with bay leaves and parsley. Alternatively, pour warm melted butter over the fish or, if you prefer a sauce, try a Hollandaise and decorate with lemon waterlilies.

Trout Soup Solianka

four ½-lb. trout
4¼ cups water
1 bouquet garni
1 chicken bouillon cube
¼ cup butter
1 carrot, thinly sliced
1 branch celery, thinly sliced
1 clove garlic, crushed
¼ cup flour
1 tablespoon tomato paste
salt and pepper
juice 1 lemon
1 tablespoon chopped parsley and dill
1 tablespoon capers
6 stuffed olives, sliced

1 Clean and fillet the fish, and cut each fillet into 3 pieces. Keep the heads, bones and trimmings to make the fish stock.

2 Place the fish bones with a bouquet garni in a saucepan of water, crumble in the bouillon cube and boil for 20 minutes.

3 Heat the butter in a saucepan and sauté the sliced carrot, celery and garlic for 15 minutes. Add the flour and cook for 3 minutes. Strain off the fish stock and add to the sautéed vegetables. Stir in the tomato paste and boil for 15 minutes until the vegetables are almost soft. Add the fish and simmer for 15 minutes. Season to taste.

4 Stir in the lemon juice, chopped parsley and dill and garnish with the capers and olives. Serve with rye bread and butter.

Serves 4-6

Poached Trout

four whole trout
2 carrots, sliced
2 onions, chopped
1 branch celery, thinly sliced
bouquet garni
1 sprig mint
6 peppercorns
4¼ cups water
2 tablespoons vinegar
salt and pepper
2 lemons

1 Clean and wash the fish.

2 Make the court bouillon: place the carrots, onions, celery, bouquet garni, mint and peppercorns in a large saucepan. Add the water and vinegar and boil for 15 minutes.

Trout Soup Solianka is garnished with capers and stuffed olives. Serve each dish with a swirl of sour cream

3 Place the trout in the court bouillon and simmer for 10 minutes.

4 Cut the lemons into wedges. Arrange the poached trout on a serving dish, pour on a little court bouillon and decorate with the lemon wedges. Serve with boiled new potatoes and melted butter or Hollandaise sauce.

Serves 4

Tip: This basic recipe for court bouillon stock can be used for all poached fish.

459

1 Clean, scale and wash the salmon. Place it in a fish kettle or large pan and cover with cold water. Add sea salt and thin slices of lemon with the pith and peel removed. Simmer gently without letting the water boil for 5 minutes per lb. Let it cool in its own liquor until quite cold 2 Drain the cooked salmon 3 Carefully remove the skin with a thin-pointed knife 4 Make some aspic and, when it is almost set, coat the fish with the aspic 5 Decorate the salmon with strips and small pieces of tomato and tarragon and coat with more aspic

to fix the decorations in place. Remove the decorated salmon from the grid and place on a large serving dish **6** Surround the fish with stuffed tomatoes, stuffed eggs and parsley **7** To serve the fish, cut off fillets, parallel to the backbone, with a knife and fork **8** When all the flesh has been taken off the first side, remove the fish bones by lifting up the backbone from the tail toward the head. Cut off the remaining fillets

461

Salmon Mousse

1 lb. salmon, poached
2 tablespoons butter
$\frac{1}{4}$ cup flour
$1\frac{1}{4}$ cups milk
salt and pepper
pinch paprika
1 tablespoon tomato paste
1 teaspoon anchovy paste
juice $\frac{1}{2}$ lemon
$\frac{1}{4}$ cup dry sherry
pinch cayenne pepper
$1\frac{1}{4}$ cups whipped heavy cream

For the Aspic:
$1\frac{1}{4}$ cups water
$\frac{1}{2}$ cup gelatin
1 chicken bouillon cube
juice $\frac{1}{2}$ lemon

For decoration:
$\frac{1}{4}$ cucumber, sliced
12 cooked peeled, deveined shrimp
6 stuffed olives

1 Remove the bones and skin from the salmon. Chop the flesh.

2 Heat the butter in a saucepan, add the flour and cook for 2 minutes. Stir in the milk.

3 Place the chopped salmon in the sauce and cook for 10 minutes. Season with salt and pepper and a pinch of paprika. Stir in the tomato paste, anchovy paste, lemon juice, sherry and cayenne pepper. Simmer for 8 minutes. Blend or pass through a food mill. Allow the salmon purée to cool a little and stir in the whipped cream.

4 Make the aspic. Boil the water and stir in and dissolve the gelatin, bouillon cube and lemon juice. Simmer for 5 minutes and allow to cool a little.

5 Stir half of the aspic into the salmon purée.

6 Cover the base of a 5-cup mold with aspic, $\frac{1}{8}$ inch thick, and allow to set. Then line the sides of the mold with aspic and set.

7 Dip the decorative garnishes — the cucumber, shrimp and olives — in a little tepid aspic and arrange inside the mold on the bottom and sides in an attractive pattern. Allow to set and then dab with the remaining aspic. Allow to set.

8 Pour in the salmon purée and chill in the refrigerator for 2 hours.

9 Stand the mold on a plate and hold under running, slightly tepid tap water. Gently loosen the mold and ease off. Be careful not to use excessive force or the mousse will fall apart.

10 Garnish with sliced cucumber, shrimp and olives.

Serves 6

Savory Pike with Walnuts

2 lbs. whole pike, or salmon
salt and pepper
$\frac{1}{2}$ cup flour
$\frac{1}{4}$ cup oil
1 cup celery, sliced
1 cup carrots, sliced
1 cup onions, sliced
$1\frac{1}{4}$ cups mushrooms, sliced
$\frac{3}{4}$ cup walnuts, chopped
$\frac{2}{3}$ cup dry white vermouth
$\frac{2}{3}$ cup water
1 chicken bouillon cube
1 cup grated cheese

1 Preheat the oven to 400°F.

2 Clean the fish and cut either into small pieces across the bone or into steaks. Season with salt and pepper and dredge with flour.

3 Heat the oil in a skillet and brown the fish for 5 minutes on each side. Place the fish pieces in a shallow, ovenproof dish.

4 In the same skillet sauté the celery, carrots, onions and mushrooms for 4 minutes. Pour the sautéed vegetables over the fish pieces and sprinkle with the walnuts. Add the vermouth and water and crumble in the bouillon cube.

5 Bake in the oven for 20 minutes. Remove and sprinkle with the grated cheese. Place under a hot broiler until brown and bubbling and serve immediately.

Serves 4

Carp in Mandarin Sauce

2 lbs. carp or catfish
1 green pepper, seeded and cut into strips
1 sweet red pepper, seeded and cut into strips
$2\frac{1}{2}$ cups court bouillon (see page 459)
1 small can mandarin oranges
dash Tabasco sauce
1 tablespoon tomato paste
$\frac{1}{4}$ cup sugar
salt and pepper
$1\frac{1}{2}$ tablespoons cornstarch
$\frac{1}{3}$ cup light cream
1 teaspoon horseradish
4 sprigs watercress

1 Preheat the oven to 400°F.

2 Clean, wash and fillet the carp.

3 Place the fish fillets in a shallow, ovenproof dish. Cover with the pepper strips and pour in the court bouillon.

4 Open the can of mandarin oranges, strain off the juice into a bowl, retaining the sections for decoration, and blend in the Tabasco, tomato paste and sugar. Season with salt and pepper. Pour over the fish and bake in the oven for 25 minutes.

5 Drain off the fish liquor, transfer the cooked fish to a clean serving dish and keep hot. Boil the liquor to reduce it by half.

6 Mix together the cornstarch and light cream and stir into the reduced fish liquor. Add the horseradish and heat through.

7 Decorate the fish with the sections of mandarin oranges and sprigs of watercress. Serve the sauce separately.

Salmon Mousse is ideal for lunch on hot, summer days or as a mouth-watering dish for any dinner party

Serves 4

Salmon Steaks with Spinach

6 tablespoons butter
2 carrots, thinly sliced
2 onions, thinly sliced
2 branches celery, thinly sliced
4 salmon steaks

For the Court Bouillon:
1 onion, cut into quarters
1 branch celery, thinly sliced
few sprigs parsley
1 carrot, thinly sliced
$\frac{1}{2}$ bay leaf
1 lb. fish trimmings
$\frac{1}{2}$ cup dry white wine
$2\frac{1}{4}$ cups water
salt and pepper

For the Spinach Purée:
2 tablespoons butter
2 lbs. spinach leaves, washed and
  coarsely chopped
salt and pepper
pinch grated nutmeg
2 tablespoons flour
2 tablespoons light cream

1 To make the court bouillon, place the onion, celery, parsley, carrot, bay leaf, fish trimmings, white wine and water in a large saucepan. Season with salt and pepper and boil for 20 minutes.

2 Heat the butter in a saucepan and sauté the sliced vegetables over low heat for 8 minutes, until soft.

3 Strain off the court bouillon. Place the salmon steaks on top of the sautéed vegetables and cover with the court bouillon. Simmer for 15 minutes.

4 Make the spinach purée: heat the butter in a sauté pan and sauté the spinach for 10 minutes, covered, over low heat. Season with salt, pepper and nutmeg.

5 Sprinkle with the flour and stir in the cream. Simmer for several minutes.

6 Remove the skin and bones from the salmon steaks and arrange on a large serving dish. Arrange the spinach purée on one side of the dish, and the sautéed vegetables on the other. Garnish the salmon steaks with thin strips of carrot and lemon slices. Serve with a Hollandaise or shrimp sauce.

Serves 4

Tips: Fish trimmings may be bought from a fish store. Alternatively, buy 1 lb. of a cheap white fish.

Sorrel makes an excellent substitute for spinach.

Crayfish Bordelaise

36 crayfish (shrimp may be
  substituted)
2 carrots, diced
2 onions, chopped
4 shallots, chopped
juice $\frac{1}{2}$ lemon
$\frac{1}{4}$ lb. butter
sprig of thyme
$\frac{1}{2}$ bay leaf
bouquet garni
$1\frac{1}{2}$ cups mushrooms, chopped
salt and pepper
pinch cayenne pepper
pinch paprika
3 tablespoons brandy
$\frac{2}{3}$ cup dry white wine
$1\frac{1}{4}$ cups water
1 chicken bouillon cube
3 tablespoons cornstarch
1 cup light cream
$1\frac{1}{2}$ tablespoons tomato paste
1 tablespoon parsley, chopped

1 Clean and gut the crayfish. Gently twist and pull out the fin from under the tail.

2 Sprinkle the chopped carrots, onions and shallots with lemon juice.

3 Heat $\frac{1}{4}$ cup butter in a sauté pan. Add the chopped vegetables, thyme and bay leaf and cook over low heat (with the lid on).

4 Meanwhile, heat the remaining butter and sauté the chopped mushrooms.

5 Add the crayfish to the sautéed vegetables and season with salt and pepper, cayenne pepper and paprika. Sauté briskly over high heat, stirring frequently, until the crayfish have turned red all over.

6 Add the brandy, sautéed mushrooms, wine and water. Crumble in the bouillon cube and cook for 15 minutes over moderate heat. Then drain the crayfish, arrange in a deep serving dish and keep hot.

7 Boil the sauce to reduce it by half. Blend the cornstarch with a little cream and stir into the reduced sauce. Add the remainder of the cream and the tomato paste. Boil for a few minutes over high heat. Correct the seasoning.

8 Pour the sauce over the crayfish, sprinkle with chopped parsley and serve.

Serves 6

Tips: All crustaceans such as lobster and large shrimp can be cooked in a similar manner. It is the shell — not the flesh — which gives the sauce its distinctive flavor. The sauce can be made into a bisque, a kind of shellfish soup, by mixing it with béchamel or velouté sauce and adding lobster meat or shrimp and so on. Crayfish Bordelaise may be served as an appetizer or as a main dish. The usual accompaniment is boiled rice.

Salmon Steaks with Spinach are garnished with spinach purée and sautéed vegetables and served with a Hollandaise sauce

Look 'n Cook Crayfish Bordelaise

1 Wash the crayfish thoroughly, changing the water several times. Devein the crayfish by breaking back the tail and removing the thin, black intestine **2** Heat some butter in a skillet and sauté the chopped carrots, onions and shallots with some thyme and a bay leaf **3** Sauté the crayfish in a mixture of oil and butter in a pan until they are red all over **4** Add the sautéed vegetables to the pan containing the crayfish **5** Season with salt and pepper, cayenne and paprika. Pour in the brandy and ignite, if you wish **6** Add the wine and water, sautéed

mushrooms and crumble in a bouillon cube. Cook for 15 minutes over moderate heat **7** Remove the crayfish from the pan, arrange in a deep serving dish and keep hot. Boil the sauce to reduce it by half. Blend some cornstarch with a little cream and stir into the reduced sauce. Add the remaining cream and tomato paste. Boil for several minutes until the sauce thickens and check seasoning **8** Pour on the crayfish

Fish Dumplings

Forcemeats are usually made from ground white fish, such as cod, and combined with breadcrumbs or a thick white sauce, egg yolks and seasonings. Shellfish can also be used but if you want to economize, mix it with a cheaper fish. Use the forcemeat for stuffing whole fish or paupiettes or shape into dumplings, cover with fish stock and poach for 10 minutes. Serve the dumplings hot as a garnish for fish dishes or cold as an hors d'oeuvre.

Basic Fish Forcemeat

1 lb. ground white fish
⅔ cup thick white sauce
¼ cup butter, softened
salt and pepper
pinch grated nutmeg
2 eggs, beaten
juice ½ lemon

1 Pound the ground fish to a paste with a rolling pin or blend.

2 Add the thick white sauce and butter and blend well. Season with salt and pepper and nutmeg.

3 Beat in the eggs and then add the lemon juice.

4 Use as a stuffing for fish or shape into dumplings and poach.

Serves 4

Tip: Serve the dumplings with a sauce. Wine or shellfish flavored sauces such as shrimp or lobster sauces are delicious.

Dumplings are an ideal way of using up leftover fish, or making a little fish go a long way. Any fish can be used.

Quenelles

1 lb. raw white fish
¼ cup butter
1 cup + 2 tablespoons flour
½ cup water
salt and pepper
pinch grated nutmeg
2 egg whites
1¼ cups heavy cream
1¼ cups fish stock
1 tablespoon chopped parsley

1 Skin and bone the fish and grind the fish flesh twice.

2 Melt the butter in a pan, add the flour and cook the mixture for 3 minutes, stirring continuously. Add the water and mix well to form a stiff paste. Cool.

3 Add the ground fish to the paste and either pound with a rolling pin or blend.

4 Season with salt and pepper and grated nutmeg and mix in the egg whites. Chill the mixture thoroughly by placing in the refrigerator or freezer.

5 When the mixture is icy cold, blend in the cream and shape the mixture into quenelles. Take a spoonful at a time and, using two spoons, shape the mixture until it is oval.

6 Place the quenelles in a large, buttered pan or baking dish. Cover with the fish stock — the quenelles should be totally immersed.

7 Bring the stock to a boil, and then simmer on top of the stove for 10 minutes until the quenelles are cooked.

8 Place the quenelles in a shallow serving dish and cover with Nantua sauce (see page 470). Sprinkle with chopped parsley and serve with boiled rice or duchesse potatoes.

Serves 6

Mushroom Fish Stuffing

½ lb. ground white fish, e.g., cod, haddock
4 soft herring roe
1½ cups fresh breadcrumbs
⅓ cup milk
¼ cup butter
¼ cup shallots, chopped
⅓ cup dry white wine
1¼ cups mushrooms, chopped
1 tablespoon chopped parsley
salt and pepper
2 eggs, beaten
juice ½ lemon

1 Blend the ground fish with the soft herring roe, breadcrumbs and milk. Grind again or place in a blender and blend.

2 Melt the butter in a pan and sweat the shallots for 2 minutes with the lid on. Add the wine and chopped mushrooms, and boil for 3 minutes.

3 Pour onto the fish mixture and stir in the chopped parsley and salt and pepper. Blend well and gradually add the eggs and lemon juice until all the moisture has been absorbed by the breadcrumbs and fish. If the mixture is too moist, add more crumbs — it should be of a firm, but moist consistency.

4 Use as a stuffing for fish or poach as dumplings.

Serves 4

Tip: Use this mushroom fish stuffing in savory, stuffed crêpes. Make the crêpes and roll up the stuffing inside. Cover with a cheesy Mornay sauce, sprinkle with grated cheese and place under a hot broiler until the crêpes are bubbling and golden-brown.

Quenelles are delicious fish dumplings, usually served in a Nantua sauce with plain, boiled rice

Nantua Sauce

2 bay leaves
large sprig thyme
½ lb. butter
1 large carrot, diced
1 large onion, diced
2 shallots, diced
handful parsley, chopped
24 small crayfish or medium
 shrimp
½ cup brandy
1 cup dry white wine
salt
cayenne pepper
2¼ cups milk
7 tablespoons flour
¾ cup light cream

1 Rub the bay leaves and the thyme between the hands.

2 Melt 4 tablespoons of the butter in a large pan. Add the carrot, onion, shallots and herbs and cook over low heat for 4-5 minutes while mixing with a wooden spoon.

3 Wash the crayfish or shrimp and remove the black vein, then add to the vegetables. Cook over high heat.

4 When the crayfish are red, sprinkle brandy over and ignite. Douse the flames with the white wine and then boil for 2 minutes. Add ½ cup water, salt and cayenne pepper. Let it cook for 10 minutes.

5 While it is cooking, prepare a white sauce: bring the milk to a boil. Meanwhile, heat 3 tablespoons of the butter, add the flour and mix it over low heat without letting it color. Cool.

6 Pour in the boiling milk and mix with a whisk. Add a little salt and let this sauce cook for 5 minutes.

7 When the crayfish or shrimp are cooked, lift them from the pan and peel the tails from the bodies. Remove the shells and put aside.

8 Blend crayfish or shrimp and vegetables to a purée. Add the purée to the white sauce and cook it again for 10 minutes.

9 Pass the sauce through a fine sieve (strainer), pressing hard with a small spoon. If the sauce obtained is too thin, simmer it over low heat until reduced to the required consistency.

10 Pass the sauce through the strainer once again, add the cream and simmer for 5 minutes. Pound the tails in a mortar or process in a food mill. Add the crayfish tails and ½ cup of the butter, cut into small pieces. Mix carefully.

11 Keep the Nantua sauce hot in a double boiler (or over a pan of hot water) and sprinkle it with the rest of the butter chopped into little pieces. Serve the sauce with quenelles (see page 468.)

Makes 4½ cups

Tip: To incorporate the butter into the sauce in Step 10, tip the pot backward and forward.

This sauce freezes well so you can make up a large quantity and then use it as required.

Quick Nantua Sauce

⅔ cup canned lobster soup
⅔ cup white sauce
1 tablespoon tomato paste
salt and pepper
1 cup peeled shrimp

1 Mix the lobster soup with the white sauce and add the tomato paste.

2 Bring the sauce to a boil and simmer for 5 minutes. Season to taste and add the shrimp.

Makes 1¼ cups

Fish Dumplings

2 lbs. skinned white fish
¼ cup chopped onion
1 egg
½ cup fresh white breadcrumbs
1 tablespoon chopped parsley
salt and pepper
½ lb. peeled, deveined shrimp
1 cup cooked peas
½ cup canned corn
3 tablespoons diced sweet red
 pepper
3 tablespoons cornstarch

For the Sauce:
¼ cup oil
¼ cup chopped onion
2 cups water
1 chicken bouillon cube
1¼ cups orange juice
bouquet garni

1 Heat the oven to 400°F. Grind the fish with the onion and blend with the egg, breadcrumbs, parsley and seasoning.

2 Divide the mixture into small dumplings, about ¼ cup each. Place the dumplings in a casserole and add the shrimp, peas, corn and red pepper.

3 Make the sauce: heat the oil in a pan, add the onion and cook for 3 minutes or until soft. Add the water, crumbled bouillon cube, orange juice, bouquet garni and seasoning and boil for 10 minutes. Pour the sauce over the fish, cover with a lid and cook in the preheated oven for 30 minutes.

4 Strain the fish, shrimp and vegetables, reserving the fish liquor, and keep warm. Pour the fish liquor into a pan and boil for 5 minutes. Mix the cornstarch with ⅔ cup water and add to the sauce. Continue cooking until the sauce has thickened. Season to taste. Place the fish dumplings, shrimp and vegetables on a serving dish, and pour on the sauce.

Serves 6

1 The ingredients **2** Melt the butter in a large pan, add the vegetables and herbs and cook for 4-5 minutes **3** Add the crayfish and cook until red. Sprinkle over the brandy and ignite it. Douse the flames with the wine and then boil for 2 minutes. Add the water and seasoning and cook for 10 minutes. Meanwhile, make the white sauce with the butter, flour and milk **4** Lift out the crayfish and separate the tails from the bodies. Remove the shells from the tails **5** and **6** Pound the vegetable mixture and add the purée to the white sauce. Cook for 10 minutes **7** Pass the sauce through a strainer. Reduce (evaporate) if necessary and strain again **8** Add the cream and simmer for 5 minutes **9** Add the crayfish tails and the butter cut into small pieces. Mix well **10** Cut the rest of the butter into small pieces and sprinkle over

Mushrooms Stuffed with Fish-balls

6 ozs. white fish fillets
8 large white mushrooms
3 tablespoons matzo meal
3 tablespoons ground almonds
1 egg, beaten
salt and pepper
pinch sugar
pinch garlic salt
1 tablespoon chopped tarragon
  or parsley
1 small onion, grated
$\frac{1}{4}$ cup butter
juice $\frac{1}{2}$ lemon
$\frac{1}{4}$ cup flour
2 tablespoons oil
8 fried bread canapés or slices of
  buttered toast, trimmed
$\frac{1}{3}$ cup cooked, peeled, deveined
  shrimp
1$\frac{1}{4}$ cups white sauce
1 tablespoon chopped parsley

1 Preheat the oven to 400°F.

2 Grind the fish fillets. Place in a large bowl. Finely chop the mushroom stalks.

3 Mix with the fish fillets the matzo meal, ground almonds, beaten egg, salt and pepper, sugar, garlic salt, chopped tarragon, grated onion, butter, lemon juice and mushroom stalks. Combine, then grind the mixture.

4 Shape into 8 fish-balls. Dust each lightly with the flour.

5 Peel the mushroom caps and place, peeled side down, on a greased baking sheet. Brush lightly with oil. Place 1 flattened fish-ball on top of each mushroom. Brush with oil. Bake in the oven for 15-20 minutes.

6 Place each stuffed mushroom on a canapé or slice of toast, trimmed to size. Add the shrimp to the white sauce and spoon a little of the sauce over each mushroom. Sprinkle with chopped parsley. Serve immediately with the rest of the sauce.

Serves 4

472

Cured & Preserved Fish

Smoked fish are among the finest of all culinary delicacies. The flavor of smoked salmon, trout and eel is incomparable, and smoking enhances the taste of cheaper fish, such as herring (bloaters and kippers are names for smoked herring), smelts, anchovies and mackerel.

Smoking is one of the most ancient methods of preserving food, discovered when people first learned to use fire for cooking. Traditionally, the fish is hung in a special chimney or smoking chamber. Woodsmoke is used, preferably from the wood of a green, hardwood tree. Oak is excellent, and rosemary, juniper and other aromatic woods impart a subtle, delicious flavor.

The fish is turned regularly so that it is smoked evenly on all sides. Before smoking, fish is usually salted between layers of coarse salt. This helps preserve it, and removes much of the moisture. Cod roe are smoked, but caviar, salmon roe and lumpfish roe are preserved in salt, as are anchovy fillets.

Smoking, salting and drying does not preserve fish indefinitely. They must be bought and eaten quickly, like fresh fish.

Starters using smoked fish can incorporate a wide range of salad ingredients. Try potato salads, using mayonnaise or a vinaigrette dressing or a sour cream dressing. Combine eating apples with celery and walnuts in mayonnaise; orange sections, strips of red and green pepper, and black olives. Finely shredded onion, dill pickles, sweet-sour cucumber, and capers make tangy garnishes, and try a generous sprinkling of chopped, fresh herbs: dill, sweet basil, mint, tarragon or parsley.

Smoked salmon, smoked trout and smoked eel are superb if eaten, simply, with thin slices of brown bread. Accompany them with generous wedges of lemon, sea salt and freshly milled black pepper or cayenne pepper; and serve with horseradish or a prepared mustard.

Mackerel and Smoked Cod Roe Pâté

1 lb. smoked mackerel (2 large
  fish)
5 ozs. smoked cod roe
$\frac{2}{3}$ cup butter
$\frac{1}{3}$ cup heavy cream
$\frac{1}{3}$ cup medium dry sherry
1 clove garlic, peeled and crushed
1 small onion, finely chopped or
  1 scallion, chopped
juice 1 lemon
salt and pepper
pinch nutmeg

1 Skin and bone the mackerel.

2 Pound the flesh of the mackerel with the cod roe in a large bowl, using a pestle, a rolling pin, or a fork.

3 Blend in the butter, cream, sherry, garlic, onion and lemon juice. Mix well together. Season with salt and pepper and nutmeg. Serve with hot buttered toast and wedges of lemon.

Tips: Herring or other smoked fish can be substituted for mackerel. The pâté can be blended to produce a smooth consistency.

Mackerel and Smoked Cod Roe Pâté is flavored with sherry and makes an excellent appetizer. Serve with fingers of toasted bread

Salmon Plate

5-7 ozs. smoked salmon, thinly sliced

For the Sauce:
½ cup mayonnaise
½ cup plain yogurt
1 tablespoon chopped dill
1-2 teaspoons prepared mustard
1 tablespoon horseradish

For the Garnish:
a few lettuce leaves
a few sprigs dill
1 green pepper, cut in strips
lemon wedges
½ lb. canned asparagus spears

1 Make the sauce: mix the mayonnaise and yogurt, then add the chopped dill, the mustard and the horseradish.

2 Spread the sauce on the salmon slices and then roll them up. Stand each roll on a bed of lettuce leaves and garnish with a dill sprig, pepper strips, lemon wedges and asparagus spears.

Serves 4

Mackerel and Tuna Picnic Loaf

one 2-lb. sandwich loaf, 1 day old and refrigerated for 24 hours
½ cup gelatin
1¼ cups white sauce
5 ozs. tuna, drained

Salmon Plate — rolled-up smoked salmon, stuffed with a mayonnaise sauce

four ½-lb. mackerel fillets, skin and bones removed
1 cup diced cooked potato
½ cup cooked peas
½ cup diced green beans
⅓ cup corn kernels
⅓ cup diced cooked sweet red pepper
12 capers
¼ cup diced dill pickle
2 tablespoons chopped onion
salt and pepper
pinch cayenne pepper
juice and grated rind ½ lemon
⅔ cup mayonnaise

1 Cut the crust off the loaf at one end and reserve. With a long bread knife, cut around inside the crust to remove the central part and leave a crust shell. Scoop out any remaining crumbs.

2 Dissolve the gelatin in ½ cup water. Bring the white sauce to a boil, add the dissolved gelatin and simmer gently for 10 minutes until thick.

3 Grind the tuna and the mackerel fillets to obtain a smooth paste. Add the paste to the thickened sauce and blend well. Mix in the rest of the ingredients except the mayonnaise. Cool and add the mayonnaise.

4 Stand the crust shell upright, and fill it with the mixture. Replace the reserved crust, stand the loaf on a plate and transfer to the refrigerator. Leave overnight to set.

5 Place the loaf flat on a plate, and decorate with slices of egg, cucumber or tomato. To serve, cut the loaf across in slices with a bread knife dipped in hot water.

Serves 10–12

Tip: The soft bread scooped out of the center can be used as dried breadcrumbs. Dry in the oven and store in an airtight container.

Mackerel and Tuna Picnic Loaf is filled with a fish and vegetable mixture and chilled in the refrigerator — ideal for picnics

Taramasalata

¼ lb. smoked cod roe
½ cup fresh white breadcrumbs
2 tablespoons light cream
2 cloves garlic, peeled and crushed
juice 1 lemon
½ cup oil
salt and pepper
pinch paprika

1 Place the cod roe and breadcrumbs in a bowl and beat in the cream and crushed garlic.

2 Stir in the lemon juice and gradually add the oil, beating vigorously all the time until the mixture is smooth. Season with salt and pepper and a pinch of paprika and serve with pita bread.

Serves 4

Tip: You can make a delicious variation to this recipe by using ½ cup cream cheese and reducing the oil by half. Garnish with chopped parsley. Taramasalata is a traditional Greek dish and makes an ideal appetizer before a meal or can be served as a party dip. Other fish roe can be used.

Roe Puffs

1 cup + 2 tablespoons flour
pinch salt
⅔ cup lukewarm water
1 tablespoon cooking oil
½ lb. mixed soft and hard herring
 roe
1 tablespoon lemon juice
2 egg whites, stiffly beaten
deep fat or oil for frying

1 Sift together the flour and salt. Mix in the water and cooking oil to make a stiff batter.

2 Add the roe and lemon juice. Fold in the egg whites.

3 Heat the deep fat to 375°F. and drop large spoonfuls of the mixture into the hot fat. Cook the puffs for 3-5 minutes or until golden-brown and crisp. Serve immediately.

Serves 4

Ocean Pie

3 large eggplants, about ½ lb. each
salt and pepper
½ lb. smoked haddock or mackerel
 fillets
⅓ cup oil
1 onion, chopped
1 clove garlic, peeled and crushed
1 tablespoon chopped parsley
pinch ground cumin
3 tablespoons tomato paste
juice 1 lemon
4 tomatoes, skinned, seeded and
 sliced
2 tablespoons shredded almonds

1 Peel the eggplants and cut them diagonally. Sprinkle the slices with salt and leave for 20 minutes to extract the moisture. Then rinse in cold water, drain and wipe with a cloth.

2 Place the mackerel or haddock in cold water in a deep pan. Bring to a boil, then simmer for 5-8 minutes. Remove the skin and bones.

3 Preheat the oven to 400°F.

4 Heat the oil in a sauté pan. Sauté the onion for 5 minutes until soft but not brown. Add the garlic and eggplant, cover the pan with a lid and fry for 5 minutes or until eggplant is soft. Add salt and pepper, parsley and cumin.

5 Transfer the vegetables to a shallow serving dish and place the fish on top.

6 Make a stock by stirring the tomato paste into ⅔ cup hot water and adding the lemon juice and seasoning. Pour it over the pie.

7 Garnish with sliced tomato and a sprinkling of almonds and bake in the preheated oven for 20 minutes.

Serves 4

Blinis

⅔ cup water
⅔ cup milk
1½ tablespoons yeast
2 eggs, beaten
pinch salt
¾ cup all-purpose flour
¾ cup whole wheat flour
¼ cup oil
7 ozs. fish roe, smoked salmon
 pâté or any caviar
⅔ cup yogurt
few scallions, sliced

1 Heat the water and milk until lukewarm and stir in the yeast. Add the beaten eggs and salt and blend in the flours to make a smooth batter. Leave the batter for about 1 hour.

2 Beat the batter again. Heat the oil in a large skillet and for each blini drop in 2 tablespoons batter (4 can be cooked at the same time). Cook on each side.

3 Serve the blinis topped with roe and a little yogurt and garnished with scallions.

Serves 6

Blinis are traditional Russian pancakes, decorated with whipped sour cream or yogurt

Fish Salads

Anchovy Salad

5 new potatoes
⅓ cup dry white wine
salt and pepper
1 bulb fennel, thinly sliced
⅔ cup green and black olives, pitted
3 hard-boiled eggs, quartered
1½ tablespoons wine vinegar
¼ cup oil
2 shallots or 4 scallions, chopped

2 cloves garlic, peeled and crushed
24 anchovy fillets
1 tablespoon parsley, chopped

1 Boil the new potatoes in salted water. When cooked but still hot, peel and cut into slices. Place in shallow dish. Place the white wine in a small saucepan and bring to a boil. Pour on the potatoes, season with salt and pepper and let cool.

2 In a salad bowl, mix the potatoes, fennel and olives. Add the vinegar, oil, chopped shallots or

---

Anchovy Salad – anchovies, new potatoes, fennel, olives and hard-boiled eggs, tossed in French dressing, make a delicious appetizer.

scallions. Mix well. Arrange the quartered eggs and the anchovies on top. Sprinkle with the parsley.

Serves 4

Tip: Smoked herring, trout, eel or salmon may be substituted for anchovies.

Pickled Fish Escabeche

¼ cup flour
pinch salt and pepper
pinch paprika
4 small red mullet or other small fish, cleaned
oil for frying

For the Pickling Mixture:
1 onion, sliced in rings
1 carrot, grooved and thinly sliced
1 small dill pickle
1 clove garlic, peeled and crushed
½ cup wine vinegar
bouquet garni
2 fresh or dried chilies, sliced, or
  pinch cayenne
1 cup water
1 lemon, thinly sliced
sprig parsley

1 Mix together the flour and seasonings. Coat the fish in the seasoned flour.

2 Heat the oil to 375°F. in a deep fat fryer and deep fry the fish, 1 or 2 at a time, for 4 minutes. Drain and dry on absorbent paper. Place the fish on a hot shallow dish.

3 Make the pickling mixture by boiling the onion, carrot, dill pickle and garlic in the vinegar and water for 5 minutes only. Season with the bouquet garni, salt, pepper and the chilies or cayenne. Pour the pickling mixture over the fish. Cool and refrigerate for 24 hours.

4 Remove the bouquet garni. Serve the fish from the dish, and decorate with lemon slices and a sprig of parsley.

Serves 4

Mayonnaise is a traditional accompaniment to cold, poached salmon and can also be served with fish salads

---

Smoked Mackerel Salad

⅓ cup mayonnaise
1 teaspoon curry powder
1 teaspoon wine vinegar
¾ cup boiled long grain rice
½ lb. smoked mackerel fillets, cut into thin strips
3 medium tomatoes, skinned and chopped
3 branches celery, diced
salt and pepper
2 hard-boiled eggs, sliced
small bunch chopped watercress
4 sliced radishes

1 In a large bowl mix together the mayonnaise, curry powder and vinegar. Stir in the rice, mackerel fillets, tomatoes and celery. Blend well and season with salt and pepper.

2 Pile the mixture onto a flat serving platter and decorate with the hard-boiled eggs, watercress and radishes.

Serves 4

Marinated Herring Salad

½ lb. smoked herring fillets, cut into strips
juice 1 lemon
2 tablespoons oil

3 cups new potatoes, boiled and diced
2 branches celery, chopped
1 dessert apple, chopped
¼ cup mayonnaise
salt and pepper
½ lb. corn kernels, frozen and thawed, or canned and drained
pinch paprika
1 lemon, cut into wedges

1 Place the smoked herring fillets in a shallow dish. Mix together the lemon juice and the oil. Pour over the fish.

2 Mix together the potatoes, celery and apple. Blend in the mayonnaise and season with salt and pepper.

3 Add the corn to the fillets and mix well.

4 Heap the mayonnaise mixture into the center of a flat serving dish. Sprinkle with the paprika. Surround with the herring fillets and corn. Garnish with the lemon wedges.

Serves 4

Tuna Salad

1 tablespoon olive oil
1 teaspoon wine vinegar
1 teaspoon chopped parsley
salt and pepper
1 large potato, cooked and diced
12 lettuce leaves
2 tomatoes, sliced
2 hard-boiled eggs, sliced
7 ozs. tuna, drained and flaked
8 rolled anchovies
8 green or black olives

1 Mix the oil, vinegar, parsley and seasonings to make a smooth dressing. Pour over the potato dice and toss lightly.

2 Arrange the lettuce on a dish and top with the tomato slices, the potatoes and the egg slices.

3 Place the tuna on top and garnish with the rolled anchovies and the olives.

Serves 4

Salmon and Rice Pilaf

four $\frac{1}{2}$-lb. salmon steaks
4$\frac{1}{4}$ cups court bouillon (see page 459)
$\frac{1}{4}$ cup butter
5 cups boiled rice
1 tablespoon chopped dill
salt and pepper
4 ozs. cream cheese, softened

1 Poach the salmon in the court bouillon for 15 minutes.

2 Melt the butter and stir in the boiled rice, dill and seasoning.

3 Drain the salmon, place on a serving dish and pipe a rosette of cream cheese onto each steak. Serve with the dill rice.

Serves 4

Tip: In our picture, we have topped the cheese with a spoonful of caviar. An alternative would be lumpfish roe.

Salmon and Rice Pilaf — poached salmon served with a savory pilaf